AKC® OFFICIAL GUIDE TO
SPORTING DOGS

Featuring Lovable Breeds including the Golden Retriever, Labrador Retriever, Pointer, and English Setter

AMERICAN KENNEL CLUB
FOUNDED 1884

AMERICAN KENNEL CLUB

CompanionHouse
BOOKS

AKC® Official Guide to Sporting Dogs

CompanionHouse Books™ is an imprint of Fox Chapel Publishing.

Project Team
The American Kennel Club®, Inc.
Fox Chapel Publishing
　Editor: Madeline DeLuca
　Designer: Wendy Reynolds
　Indexer: Jay Kreider

All photos are credited to The American Kennel Club®, Inc, unless otherwise noted.

Additional Shutterstock.com images: Anna Averianova (1, 7 top left); Christian Mueller (5); Dora Zett (23); Glenka (101).

American Kennel Club®, AKC®, AKC Meet the Breeds®, AKC S.T.A.R. Puppy®, AKC Rally®, AKC Scent Work®, Canine Good Citizen®, and Foundation Stock Service® are registered trademarks of The American Kennel Club.

Copyright © 2025 by the American Kennel Club®

All rights reserved. No part of this book may be reproduced, stored in a retrieval system, or transmitted in any form or by any means, electronic, mechanical, photocopying, recording, or otherwise, without the prior written permission of Fox Chapel Publishing, except for the inclusion of brief quotations in an acknowledged review.

ISBN 978-1-62187-245-0

Library of Congress Control Number: 2025932130

This book has been published with the intent to provide accurate and authoritative information in regard to the subject matter within. While every precaution has been taken in the preparation of this book, the author and publisher expressly disclaim any responsibility for any errors, omissions, or adverse effects arising from the use or application of the information contained herein. The techniques and suggestions are used at the reader's discretion and are not to be considered a substitute for veterinary care. If you suspect a medical problem, consult your veterinarian.

Fox Chapel Publishing
903 Square Street
Mount Joy, PA 17552

We are always looking for talented authors.
To submit an idea, please send a brief inquiry to acquisitions@foxchapelpublishing.com.

Printed and bound in China
First Printing

A representative of the sporting breed—the Irish Water Spaniel.

Foreword

The original materials compiled in the *AKC® Stud Book* were listings of sporting dogs from 1878, and the sporting breeds have been batting leadoff in show catalogs and stud registers ever since.

The breeds of the AKC® Sporting Group—spaniels, setters, pointers, and retrievers—are the most homozygous as to function: All are used to work on feathered game alongside human hunters bearing rifles. But it was not always so; many sporting breeds, today known as "gundogs" or "bird dogs," predate the advent of firearms and were developed to find and flush birds when hunters used falcons, clubs, or nets in the field.

The breeds of the Sporting Group are subcategorized along three basic hunting styles. The flushing breeds, mostly spaniels, flush or "spring" gamebirds from their nesting areas in brush and high grass, mark where the downed bird lands, and then retrieve the prey.

The pointing and setting breeds work a great distance from the hunter and will point or set (crouch) to indicate the presence of game birds to their human hunting partner.

The retrievers specialize in waterfowl. They wait and watch until the hunter downs his target, usually a duck on the wing. They then mark the spot on the lake where the duck lands, swim out to the spot, take the game in their "soft" mouth, swim back to their human hunting partner, and deliver the game to hand. The retrievers are equipped with thick coats, allowing them to work comfortably in icy water.

Of course, not all of today's sporting dogs are working hunters. Many are simply loving and loyal family companions. The Labrador and Golden Retrievers are among the most popular pets among all dog breeds in America and around the world. The trainability, attentiveness, and eagerness to please of good bird dogs make them excellent housemates.

Contents

What Is the AKC®?	6
Anatomy of a Dog	10
Finding the Perfect Puppy	14
The Sport of Dogs	18
The Sporting Group	23
Breed Profiles	24
Index	160

Field Spaniel 73

Flat-Coated Retriever 77

German Shorthaired Pointer 81

German Wirehaired Pointer 85

Golden Retriever 89

Gordon Setter 93

Irish Red and White Setter 97

Irish Setter 100

Irish Water Spaniel 104

Labrador Retriever 108

Lagotto Romagnolo 114

Nederlandse Kooikerhondje 119

Nova Scotia Duck Tolling Retriever 123

Pointer 127

Spinone Italiano 131

Sussex Spaniel 135

Vizsla 139

Weimaraner 143

Welsh Springer Spaniel 147

Wirehaired Pointing Griffon 151

Wirehaired Vizsla 155

What Is the AKC®?

In September 1884, a group of sportsmen gathered in Philadelphia to establish an organization to govern dog shows in the United States. Each member of the group was a representative or "delegate" from a dog club that had, in the recent past, held a dog show or field trial. It was the birth of the American Kennel Club® (AKC®).

Since that historic meeting, the AKC®, a club of clubs, has blossomed into the world's largest registry of purebred dogs and the nation's leading not-for-profit organization devoted to the study, breeding, and advancement of all things canine.

From glamorous dog shows in spotlighted arenas to small obedience matches on summer afternoons, promoting the benefits of the purebred dog is the AKC®'s central focus, but it is far from the whole picture.

It's the love of dogs, in their infinite variety, that is the soul of the AKC®. The organization is dedicated to protecting the rights of breeders and dog owners, as well as promoting responsible dog ownership.

Advancing Health and Welfare

- **AKC® Canine Health Foundation (CHF):** Founded in 1995 as an independent, affiliated nonprofit organization, CHF is dedicated to advancing the health of all dogs and increasing their owners' knowledge by funding scientific research and supporting the dissemination of health information to prevent, treat, and cure canine disease.
- **AKC® Reunite:** The mission of the nation's largest nonprofit pet recovery service is to keep pet microchipping and enrollment affordable, with no annual fees, so more lost pets can find their way

Dogs fulfill countless roles in today's society, like this Wirehaired Pointing Griffon's hunting abilities.

Breeders continue to strive for perfection in their breeding programs: excellent conformation, correct temperaments, and outstanding working abilities. Consider these Irish Water Spaniels.

home. Since 1995, AKC® has helped reunite more than 600,000 lost pets with their owners. More than ten million pets (of thirty-five different species) are enrolled in the AKC® Reunite pet-recovery service. As a nonprofit, AKC® Reunite gives its profits back to the US pet community through programs including grants to support volunteer canine search and rescue organizations, microchip scanner donations to shelters and rescues, and the AKC® Pet Disaster Relief trailers that deliver nonperishable necessities for sheltering pets to local emergency-management teams. These trailers provide animal-care services during the first critical hours following a disaster, before FEMA support and services can be deployed. Additionally, AKC® Reunite's Adopt a K-9 Cop grant program matches donations from AKC® clubs to provide funds for police departments to acquire a K-9 officer.
- **AKC® Humane Fund:** The AKC® Humane Fund celebrates and supports responsible dog ownership with grants, scholarships, the Awards for Canine Excellence, and other programs. Its grants for pet-friendly domestic violence shelters and breed rescue organizations advance and uphold the human-canine bond.
- **AKC® Inspections:** The AKC® is the only purebred registry in the United States with an ongoing routine kennel-inspection program. The AKC® has a dedicated team of field agents who visit kennels to help breeders while ensuring the proper care and conditions of AKC®-registered dogs and verifying that breeders are maintaining accurate records for their dogs. Since 2000, AKC® field agents have conducted over 70,000 inspections nationwide.

Building Community

The AKC® offers a wealth of education, information, and experiences for people who love dogs, including:
- **Public Events**: AKC Meet the Breeds®, its flagship event held in New York City, introduces thousands of people to new breeds, dog sports, AKC® initiatives, and activities.
- **AKC® Education**: This department strives to be the source of knowledge for all things dog, educating the public about purebred dogs, the sport of purebred dogs, and responsible dog ownership.

The AKC® Museum of the Dog in New York City has this life-size bronze Irish Setter statue, *Sky*, on display. The statue rests on a real quilted dog bed!

AKC® Education meets this goal through online courses and exams for judges, groomers, breeders, trainers, and more via the AKC® Canine College. Additionally, AKC® Public Education offers numerous programs for the community such as the AKC® Canine Ambassador Program, AKC® PupPals, and AKC® Educator Resources. Finally, informative webinars are offered free of charge monthly on topics of interest for all dog owners.

- **Award-Winning Magazines**: *AKC® Family Dog*, published six times a year, is packed with expert advice on health, grooming, behavior, and training, as well as heartwarming and inspiring tales of dogs and their owners that you will find nowhere else. *The AKC® Gazette* features breed columns for every registered AKC® breed.
- **Website**: *AKC.org*, the organization's website, gives the public 24/7 access to the world's most extensive storehouse of knowledge on all topics related to dogs. It is also the go-to place for topnotch goods and services.
- **AKC.tv**: The digital network AKC.tv features dog-related programming 24/7, as well as an on-demand library of world-class dog events, training and health tips, and original series created especially for dog owners and lovers, such as AKC Good Dog TV.
- **The AKC® Museum of the Dog**: Founded in 1980 in New York City, this AKC® gallery is the world's finest collection of dog-related art, comprising depictions of man's best friend in oil, watercolor, ink, and sculpture.
- **The AKC® Research Library**: Founded in 1934, this library is a unique repository of dog-related books, memorabilia, and ephemera, including many rare and antique editions, modern works, bound periodicals, and stud books from all over the world. The library presently contains more than 18,000 volumes.
- **AKC® Canine Partners**: Begun in 2009, this important program is designed to promote responsible ownership of both purebred and mixed breeds. It allows mixed breeds to enter companion events, based solely on the dogs' training and performance. There are over 500,000 dogs enrolled. Mixed breeds are eligible to title in tracking and

Anatomy of a Dog

The dog is much more than the sum of his parts. Still, it's important to remember that dogs' beauty and talents—and our emotional responses to them—have been molded over at least fifteen thousand years of evolution. Beyond the evolutionary process, selective breeding created unique looks and enhanced inborn abilities and temperament, all related to how those various parts come together. Those parts and how they are assembled have created the most versatile species on earth. Today, there are dogs for all kinds of jobs, whether it's leaping out of a helicopter to save a person who is drowning or nestling into a lap to comfort the elderly. In many ways, dogs and people are very much alike, beings composed of such stuff as bone, blood, muscle, skin, and hair. Using DNA from a Boxer named Tasha, scientists created a map of the canine genome. Comparisons to the human version have shown us that, genetically speaking, there's only about a 15-percent difference between you and your dog. That's why dogs are proving to be such excellent models for scientists seeking treatments for the worst human illnesses, such as cancer, heart disease, and arthritis.

Breed Standards

Many spectators at dog shows wonder how judges, in the two-and-a-half minutes allocated to examine a dog in the ring, can pick a winner. What is the judge looking at when he or she peers into the dog's mouth, runs his or her hand along the dog's sides, and steps back and intently watches every step as the handler and the dog move around the ring? How does the judge choose one dog over another?

Judges evaluate dogs based on a written description of an ideal specimen, which is known as the breed standard. A dog who possesses all the best traits mentioned in the standard is said to have good *type*.

In an examination, the judge will go over each dog with his or her hands, checking for breed-type points, those physical characteristics that give the breed its unique shape, movement, and overall appearance.

Field Spaniels have folding ears.

It's impossible to list every anatomical point the judge will consider; there are hundreds. Butfollowing is a quick rundown of some of the highlights, as well as the terms used to describe a few variations that separate a giant, plushly coated Newfoundland from a petite, near-naked Chinese Crested.

EARS

Ears: Whether they're the oversized triangles of a Pembroke Welsh Corgi, the long, velvety flaps of the Basset Hound, or the butterfly wings that grace the head of the Papillon, ears are among the most expressive parts of the dog. The size, shape, and the ear set, (how the lobes are attached to the head) contribute a lot to the overall look. There are more than thirty terms used to describe the various canine ear shapes. Here are just a few:
- bat ear
- blunt-tipped ear
- flying ear
- folding ear

BITE

Most dogs have forty-two teeth, twenty in the upper jaw, twenty-two in the lower. When a judge looks into a dog's mouth, he or she is making sure that all the teeth are present and that the bite conforms to the breed standard. There are four basic bites, and each serves a purpose either in creating an expression or in the dog's work:
- overshot
- undershot
- level
- scissors

FRONT ASSEMBLY

The front assembly generally refers to the shoulders and the front legs. Correct form here allows the dog's legs to move out in front, what is known as reach. Ideal reach will differ between, say, a Saluki and a Bulldog, and this will be determined by the construction of the shoulders, legs, and forefeet.

Anatomical features have definitive purposes, like the soft mouth of the steadfast Curly-Coated Retriever.

12 AKC Official Guide to Sporting Dogs

Labrador Retrievers have otter tails.

Judges pay special attention to angulation, the angles of bones and joints. Angulation is one of the most important aspects of canine anatomy. Correct angulation encourages proper muscular development, which makes for a dog who can move with ease.

FEET

Dogs' feet come in several shapes:
- Cat feet, compact with a short third digit, are thought to improve endurance because they are easier to lift.
- Webbed feet are good for swimming breeds like the Newfoundland, Labrador Retriever, and Portuguese Water Dog.
- Hare feet are elongated with two center toes larger than the side toes, seen in some sighthounds and Toy breeds.

RIB CAGE

Dogs have nine pairs of true ribs (connected directly to the breastbone), three pairs of false ribs (connected together by cartilage), and a set of floating ribs (unattached, as name implies). Judges will check for spring, the curvature in the ribs, which indicates how much space there is for heart and lungs.

REAR ASSEMBLY

The rear assembly—structure of the hindquarters—contributes to the dog's ability to thrust forward with his back legs, allowing him to sprint and leap. This is known as drive. As with the front assembly, correct angulation is extremely important. Also, the front and rear must be in balance, or the dog's movement will be impaired.

TAILS

Finally, the judge will look at the tail and the tailset (how the tail is attached to the dog's rump). As with ears, there are many different types of tails, and there's a separate ideal for each breed:
- plume
- curled
- sickle
- otter
- screw

Finding the Perfect Puppy

Adding a dog to your household is a big decision, one not to be made on impulse. The right choice may enhance your life beyond all expectations, while a bad one can mean aggravation, disappointment, and heartache. So, with the millions of puppies and dogs out there, how do you pick the right one?

Make sure you research the breed of dog and the breeder carefully before committing.

If you're fortunate enough to visit your puppy at your breeder's home more than once, you'll be able to observe his progress—from mom's milk to the feeding trough to your kitchen! See these German Shorthaired Pointer puppies.

Are You Ready for a Dog?

First, it's important to ask yourself some hard questions. If you have a family that includes a spouse and children, sit down with them and ask them these questions too. Nothing is sadder than a puppy purchased on impulse because "the kids wanted a dog"—a puppy who is then relegated to the backyard when the novelty wears off.

When you start to consider owning a dog, here are some of the important lifestyle questions to ask yourself:

- Do I have time for walks, training, and daily maintenance?
- Am I prepared for the expense of dog ownership, which includes regular veterinary care, such as exams and vaccinations, as well as food, bedding, training, and toys?
- Am I willing to include the dog in my life? Dogs are highly social creatures. They do best when they are actively involved in as much of their human's life as possible. A dog will not be happy sitting home all day while his people are at work, then getting a brief walk before a long night home alone again because his people like to go out after work.
- Can I make a commitment to the average ten- to twenty-year life span of most dogs?

Pick Your Breed

If you answer yes to all these questions, you next need to determine which breed of dog is best for you. That can be achieved by asking yourself how you hope to include a dog in your life:

- Are you a marathon runner looking for a jogging buddy or are you a couch potato who wants a pal to join you watching TV?
- Do you mind having to vacuum every day?
- Are you interested in getting involved in such sports as agility, field trials, or conformation dog showing?
- Would you prefer a dog who reflects your heritage?
- Do you have young children in the house?

Breeders seek to produce litters stamped with unmistakable breed type, consistent soundness, and excellent temperaments. Consider the beauty of these English Cocker Spaniels.

These are just a few of the questions that you should ask yourself in narrowing down the right breed for you. Think about every aspect of your life and consider how your dog should fit in.

Choose Your Breeder

Once you settle on a breed, you come to the next and most important step—finding that perfect puppy. When you start your search, the most often-repeated bit of advice you'll hear is: "Go to a responsible breeder."

Many people, though, don't know how to do that, or even what the term really means. You can't just walk up to a person selling puppies and say, "Are you a responsible breeder?" The answer, of course, will be "YES!"

Before you start looking, you need to understand the real meaning of the words "responsible" or "reputable" breeder and how you can distinguish between that person and someone just out to make a buck, or someone who may be well-meaning but hasn't the time, energy, or experience to breed quality puppies. It is not simply a matter of putting two nice dogs together and hoping for the best.

What Is a Responsible Breeder?

Dog breeding is both science and art. A breeder must know all about canine genetics and anatomy, nutrition, and psychology, both canine and human. He or she must know how to read a pedigree to choose sires and dams who will produce beautiful puppies, healthy and sound in both body and mind. The breeder must know the history of the breed, what role these dogs have played through the years, and how that role may be changing in the modern world. He or she must have what is known as "an eye for a dog," an ability to see which dogs in a litter have the physical attributes to be a great example of a breed. The breeder must have a solid background in training and dog behavior, the knowhow to size up a litter and say which puppy has the mental and emotional makeup to someday become a natural show dog, an agility champ, or a great pet.

It's impossible to pick this up overnight. Decades of dedication and experience, learning what works and doesn't, go into dog breeding. Some of the breeders you meet may have whelped their first litters before you were born. And, if you are going to a new breeder, that person will likely have a mentor, a more experienced breeder who has shared knowledge with the newcomer.

The best breeders will be intensely involved in the dog world. You will see them at shows and dog-sport events. They are passionate about their breed and its welfare, from the Best in Show ring to rescue. It is not unusual to find some of the top show breeders devoting hours to helping a member of their canine clan who may have fallen on hard times. Some will drive all night to rescue a dog who somehow wound up in a shelter. They love dogs, and they love their breed, sometimes to a point that might seem odd to a newcomer to this world.

Green Light or Red Flag?

So, how can you know whether or not someone offering you a puppy is a responsible breeder? The following is a checklist of green lights, qualities that suggest you are in the hands of someone worthy of that description. We also present red flags that will suggest you should look elsewhere for your new family member.

 ## GREEN LIGHT

- The breeder is affiliated with the AKC®, may be an AKC® Breeder of Merit program participant, and may be connected to the AKC® parent club for the breed.

- The breeder eagerly opens his or her home to you. By visiting, you'll get an idea of how the puppy is being raised, and what the mother is like in both looks and temperament.

- The breeder should be aware of breed-specific genetic tests that may identify inheritable health issues, if any are available.

- A breeder will ask you to fill out a questionnaire, sometimes several pages long, and may insist on a series of conversations, on the phone and face-to-face.

- The breeder can show you pedigree information—AKC® registration documents for the sire, dam, and litter. The words "American Kennel Club®" and the AKC® logo should be clearly visible on these documents.

 ## RED FLAG

- A breeder, unaffiliated with any club or organization, who offers no background on the puppy's parents or grandparents.

- The breeder does not allow you into his or her home or, worse, wants to meet you in a parking lot or some other public place.

- A breeder who will not show you any health-screening results, talk about the health issues encountered, or says he or she does not conduct any health or genetic tests because he or she has "never had a problem."

- A breeder who is only interested in whether you can afford the asking price.

- No papers of any kind are offered, there is a charge for registration papers, or the registration papers are from a registry other than the American Kennel Club®. Look carefully at the application because some alternative registries choose names that are very similar to the AKC®, but they are not the real thing.

The Sport of Dogs

The arena grows dark and hushed, spotlights dance, and a deep voice comes over a loudspeaker. "We highly encourage you to cheer on your favorites," he urges the crowd, but the spectators need little prodding. They are already shouting the names of the group winners, jumping to their feet to cheer and applaud as, one by one, the best dogs in the country breeze onto the floor.

Thousands of eyes are on the seven glittering, perfectly groomed dogs and their handlers moving in a graceful circle around the carpeted floor. It is the moment of truth, the selection of the top dog, Best in Show, at a major event.

When people think of the sport of dogs, this is what often comes to mind, and for good reason. Such events have been a part of the American landscape since before there was a Brooklyn Bridge or electric lights, when the Westminster Kennel Club held its first bench show in 1877. Seven years later, the founding of the American Kennel Club® opened the country's great age of the dog show.

In the years since, there's been an explosion of sports for four-footed competitors. Today there is something for everyone. Got a Papillon that flies over the furniture? Try agility. Your retriever hangs on your every word? Try obedience, where being a really good dog is a competitive sport. Got a fuzzy shovel who has turned your garden upside down? Earthdog! A hound who chases anything that moves? Lure coursing! A sheepdog who gathers everyone in the house into one corner? Herding! A Bloodhound who can't get his nose off the ground? Mantrailing or tracking!

AKC® sports and activities fall into five categories: dog shows (conformation), companion events, performance events, the Family Dog Program, and the Title Recognition Program.

Name your dog's passion, and there's an AKC® activity for it. The opportunities for fun and frolic are endless. In the following pages, we'll introduce you to just a few of the many sports and activities AKC® has to offer. For more details on rules, regulations, and titles, visit the AKC® website, *www.akc.org*.

The AKC® National Championship has become one the nation's most prestigious and exciting dog shows, usually attracting the largest entries of the year.

The AKC® National Championship not only offers breed classes for all recognized breeds but also features a junior-handling competition, shown here.

Conformation

The signature event held under AKC® rules is the dog show, also known as a conformation event. Judges evaluate a dog's conformation, which means how the dog's physical structure and temperament compare to the breed standard, the blueprint of an ideal representative.

WHO MAY PARTICIPATE?

For conformation shows, a dog must:
- Be individually registered with the American Kennel Club®
- Be six months of age or older
- Be a breed for which classes are offered at the show
- Be unaltered. Spayed or neutered dogs are not eligible to compete in conformation classes because the purpose of a dog show is to evaluate breeding stock. One exception to this rule is in Junior Showmanship, where spayed and neutered dogs can be shown.

Children of All Ages

One thing that strikes first-timers to an AKC® event is the great range in the ages among the human participants. It is not unusual to see teenage handlers competing against people old enough to be their grandparents. Age in the competitive dog world is truly just a number, and among the great joys of being part of it are the friendships that leap across the generation gap. From nine to ninety, pick up a show lead, and you have something in common.

The AKC®'s Junior Showmanship program is designed to help youngsters gain dog show experience in conformation. These classes are open to juniors from nine to eighteen years old and are aimed at helping young dog lovers develop handling skills and learn about good sportsmanship, dogs, and dog shows. There are additional opportunities for youngsters in companion and performance events. These programs offer young people direction if they are considering careers that involve dogs, along with a solid foundation for a lifetime of loving canine companions.

Agility

"Addictive" is the word most participants use to describe this fast-paced sport, which was launched in England in the late 1970s. It was invented as a kind of a half-time entertainment during the annual Crufts dog show, with obstacles based on equestrian competitions. The popularity of the sport soared after its introduction in the United States in the 1980s.

Agility tests a team's skill at negotiating a complex course composed of jumps, tunnels, and other obstacles. Border Collies, Shetland Sheepdogs, and other herding breeds rule here, but you'll see all kinds, from squat Bulldogs to majestic Great Danes, as well as mixed breeds, dashing around the courses.

Obedience

This is a chance to show off how well you and your dog work together as a team by performing a series of obedience exercises that are scored by a judge. At the most fundamental level, teams are judged on how well they perform the simple commands that every dog should know—sit, down, heel, and stay. You can start with informal matches, held by local dog clubs, and then progress to formal AKC® competitions. There are several levels, each with more advanced skills and challenging exercises.

Tracking

Dogs are geniuses when it comes to following their noses, which are thousands of times more sensitive than those of humans. A puppy instinctively uses his nose—training your dog to track simply hones his natural ability. And since all dogs have a natural ability to follow a scent, any breed is capable of learning to track. Tracking requires very little equipment. You just need a harness, a 20- to- 40-foot lead, a few flags to mark your track, and an open grassy area free of obstacles, such as roads, ditches, or woods.

AKC Scent Work®

AKC Scent Work® is a sport that mimics the task of working detection dogs—such as drug dogs or explosives dogs—in finding a specific scent and communicating to the handler that the scent has been found. In Scent Work, the dog-handler teams are placed in a search area in which a target odor (such as an essential oil) has been hidden out of sight. Each dog must use nothing but his sense of smell to

Obedience trials have been around since the 1930s and continue to be regarded as the proving grounds of dog trainers. See this German Shorthaired Pointer.

Retriever field trials test a retriever's ability to mark a bird and retrieve it.

locate the hide, and the handler must trust when the dog has found it, confidently calling out "alert!" to the judge. Scent-work searches are conducted in a variety of everyday environments; for example, in a scent-work trial, a dog might be asked to find the odor in a collection of luggage, in a classroom, around a baseball dugout, or buried up to 6 inches beneath the ground. All purebred dogs and mixed breeds are eligible to participate in AKC Scent Work®.

Field Trials and Hunting Tests

Sporting-breed field trials are open to registered pointing breeds, retrievers, and spaniels, including those with PAL/ILP numbers. These breeds also are eligible for hunting tests. The sports are designed to show how well a dog can help a hunter find and retrieve game.

In field trials, dogs compete against one another for placements and points toward their championships.

In hunting tests, the dog's ability to perform is judged against a standard of performance established by the regulations. Hunting tests and field trials have different levels of difficulty and require dogs to mark multiple birds and, at higher levels, find unmarked birds (called blind retrieves), following the handler's instructions.

In pointing-breed field trials and hunting tests, dogs run in pairs around a course on which birds are liberated. The dogs demonstrate their ability to find birds, point staunchly, and retrieve downed birds. Retrievers are tested on their ability to remember (mark) the location of downed birds and return those birds to their handlers. Retriever events also test a dog's ability to find unmarked birds (called blind retrieves). Spaniels are judged on their natural and trained ability to hunt, flush, and retrieve game on both land and water.

The Weimaraner competes in tracking events.

AKC Rally®

In rally, dog-and-handler teams negotiate a course of exercises following sequentially numbered signs, known as stations. Each team progresses from sign to sign at its own pace, performing exercises that are written in pictographs on the signs.

Unlike obedience, where commands may be given only once and handlers may not verbally encourage their dogs, in rally it is fine to praise the dog throughout your run. Judges score the teams on how accurately they perform the exercises and how well they work together.

Fast CAT®

The Fast CAT® event presents dogs with a straight-line 100-yard dash. The dog's time is converted to miles per hour (mph), and they earn points based on their mph to earn titles. The best of the best are showcased on the AKC® website, which ranks the top twenty fastest dogs by breed.

Canine Good Citizen®/S.T.A.R. Puppy®

Every dog, mixed or purebred, can earn the Canine Good Citizen® (CGC) title, demonstrating that he has the manners and skills to live in polite society. Since the CGC program began, more than one million dogs have earned the CGC award. The CGC test consists of ten items. Some, like accepting a friendly stranger and walking through a crowd, are simply benchmarks of good manners. Other items test basic skills, such as sit, down, stay, and come when called. Once dogs pass the CGC, they can move on for a more advanced title, AKC® Community Canine (CGCA). Dogs also have an opportunity to earn the AKC® Urban CGC™ (CGCU) title if they can pass a test with challenges unique to a city environment.

The S.T.A.R. Puppy® Program sets a youngster up for success in later activities by providing the basics for a good dog. S.T.A.R. stands for "Socialization, Training, Activity, and a Responsible Owner," which are the cornerstones for a happy, well-behaved pup.

The Sporting Group

Sporting dogs are naturally active and alert, making them likeable, well-rounded companions. Originally developed to work closely with hunters to locate and retrieve quarry, these dogs excel in various field activities. There are four types of AKC® sporting dogs: pointers, setters, spaniels, and retrievers. Known for their superior instincts in both water and woods, many of these breeds thrive in hunting and other outdoor pursuits.

Many sporting dogs, especially those bred for water retrieval, have well-insulated, water-repellent coats that are resilient to the elements. If you're considering getting one, keep in mind that most sporting dogs require regular, invigorating exercise to stay happy and healthy.

Some of the most popular sporting breeds are the Labrador Retriever, the Weimaraner, the Irish Setter, and the Golden Retriever. Buddy, the Golden Retriever from the movie *Air Bud*, is a shining example of the sporting group: lovable, intelligent, and active.

A Flat-Coated Retriever; an easy-to-train, responsive dog.

Meet the American Water Spaniel

Recognized by AKC® in 1940
American Water Spaniel Club (americanwaterspanielclub.org), formed in 1985

Traits
- Strong-Willed
- Eager
- Happy

HISTORY

The American Water Spaniel, developed in the mid- to late 1800s in the Midwest, is one of the few breeds truly "born in the U.S.A." Bred out of necessity by frontier settlers, the dog was an all-around meat hunter, having no preference for fur or feathers. The hunters of that era were especially fond of the AWS because of his smaller size and unmatched tenacity for retrieving game. The breed is versatile, powerful, and sturdy enough to handle the large marshes and harsh conditions of the upper Midwest, yet small enough to enter and exit skiffs with ease. The precise origin of the AWS is unknown. Most enthusiasts agree that the old English Water Spaniel (now extinct), the Curly-Coated Retriever, and the Irish Water Spaniel are among its ancestors. The AKC® recognized the AWS in 1940 through the efforts of Dr. F. J. Pfeiffer, New London, Wisconsin. In 1986, legislation was passed making the AWS Wisconsin's official state dog. Being a versatile dog, the AWS does not exactly fit as a flushing spaniel or a retriever.

Because of these characteristics, the American Water Spaniel Club (AWSC), the AKC® parent club, in 1986 created its own unique working certificate tests designed to demonstrate both flushing and retrieving abilities. In 2005, the parent club voted to classify the AWS as a flushing spaniel, thus allowing the breed to earn AKC® hunt test titles provided dogs complete additional AWSC retrieving work. In April 2011, after being petitioned by the AWSC, the AKC® allowed the AWS to earn retriever titles, which eliminated the AWSC retrieving requirement. Today, the AWS is one of a handful of breeds allowed by the AKC® to acquire both spaniel and retriever titles. Unlike some other sporting breeds, the AWS does not have show lines and field lines. Many AWS have both conformation and field titles.

FORM AND FUNCTION

The AWS is a lot of dog in a small package! He is expected to flush and retrieve a variety of game in varied terrain and conditions, and yet he is small enough to fit in a skiff or canoe. To that end, a robust dog with well-sprung ribs and muscling to perform in tough cover and cold water is required. A dense coat and extra subcutaneous fat protection sets the AWS apart from other sporting spaniels. The moderately feathered, rocker-shaped tail is used as a rudder to facilitate swimming.

LIVING WITH AN AMERICAN WATER SPANIEL

When meeting a litter of puppies, look for a good bite, a full dense coat, and strong muscle and bone. A puppy should be outgoing and inquisitive; at eight weeks he should already show willingness to seek out and retrieve a toy. Temperament is an important quality to determine the dog he will become. Ideal AWS owners are active people who have had prior experience raising and training dogs. This loyal and affectionate dog can be strong-willed, requiring a strong leader. Because the AWS is intelligent and prone to boredom if unchallenged, obedience training for a new puppy makes for a happy owner and a loyal companion. These dogs are food motivated, so treats are helpful for early training. Moderate brushing and clipping maintain a healthy coat and pleasing appearance and at the same time reduce shedding. Routine cleaning of the ear canals prevents infections and inflammation. Most AWS live a healthy life to the age of ten to thirteen years. As they become elderly, arthritis may result from their active lifestyle, and pain symptoms may not be recognized because of their high tolerance for discomfort. The AWS is a dog with an innate sense of fair play, a great comical nature, incredible hunting instincts, and a strong devotion to his family.

COMPETITION

The AWSC supports annual national specialties for conformation and performance events, which include obedience, rally, working certificates, and other field events. The parent club also sponsors AKC® spaniel hunting tests. In addition, the AWS participates in a variety of other competitive sports including tracking, agility, barn hunting, flyball, and retriever hunting tests. The nice disposition of the AWS makes for an excellent therapy dog who can meet emotional needs as well.

Official Standard for the American Water Spaniel

General Appearance: The American Water Spaniel was developed in the United States as an all-around hunting dog, bred to retrieve from skiff or canoes and work ground with relative ease. The American Water Spaniel is an active muscular dog, medium in size with a marcel to curly coat. Emphasis is placed on proper size and a symmetrical relationship of parts, texture of coat and color.

Size, Proportion, Substance: *Size*—15 to 18 inches for either sex. Males weighing 30 to 45 pounds. Females weighing 25 to 40 pounds. Females tend to be slightly smaller than the males. There is no preference for size within the given range of either sex providing correct proportion, good substance and balance is maintained. *Proportion*—Is slightly longer than tall, not too square or compact. However, exact proportion is not as important as the dog being well-balanced and sound, capable of performing the breed's intended function. *Substance*—A solidly built and well-muscled dog full of strength and quality. The breed has as much substance and bone as necessary to carry the muscular structure but not so much as to appear clumsy.

Head: The head must be in proportion to the overall dog. Moderate in length. *Expression* is alert, self-confident, attractive and intelligent. Medium size *eyes* set well apart, while slightly rounded, should not appear protruding or bulging. Lids tight, not drooping. Eye color can range from a light yellowish brown to brown, hazel or of dark tone to harmonize with coat. Disqualify yellow eyes. Yellow eyes are a bright color like that of lemon, not to be confused with the light yellowish brown. *Ears* set slightly above the eye line but not too high on the head, lobular, long and wide with leather extending to nose. *Skull* rather broad and full, *stop* moderately defined, but not too pronounced. *Muzzle* moderate in length, square with good depth. No inclination to snipiness. The lips are clean and tight without excess skin or flews. Nose dark in color, black or dark brown. The nose sufficiently wide and with well-developed nostrils to insure good scenting power. *Bite* either scissor or level.

Neck, Topline, Body: *Neck* round and of medium length, strong and muscular, free of throatiness, set to carry head with dignity, but arch not accentuated. *Topline* level or slight, straight slope from withers. *Body* well-developed, sturdily constructed but not too compactly coupled. Well-developed brisket extending to elbow neither too broad nor too narrow. The ribs well-sprung, but not so well-sprung that they interfere with the movement of the front assembly. The loins strong, but not having a tucked-up look. *Tail* is moderate in length, curved in a rocker fashion, can be carried either slightly below or above the level of the back. The tail is tapered, lively and covered with hair with moderate feathering.

Forequarters: Shoulders sloping, clean and muscular. Legs medium in length, straight and well-boned but not so short as to handicap for field work or so heavy as to appear clumsy. Pasterns strong with no suggestion of weakness. Toes closely grouped, webbed and well-padded. Size of feet to harmonize with size of dog. Front dewclaws are permissible.

Hindquarters: Well-developed hips and thighs with the whole rear assembly showing strength and drive. The hock joint slightly rounded, should not be small and sharp in contour, moderately angulated. Legs from hock joint to foot pad moderate in length, strong and straight with good bone structure. Hocks parallel.

Coat: Coat can range from marcel (uniform waves) to closely curled. The amount of waves or curls can vary from one area to another on the dog. It is important to have undercoat to provide sufficient density to be of protection against weather, water or punishing cover, yet not too coarse or too soft. The throat, neck

and rear of the dog well-covered with hair. The ear well-covered with hair on both sides with ear canal evident upon inspection. Forehead covered with short smooth hair and without topknot. Tail covered with hair to tip with moderate feathering. Legs have moderate feathering with waves or curls to harmonize with coat of dog. Coat may be trimmed to present a well-groomed appearance; the ears may be shaved; but neither is required.

Color: Color either solid liver, brown or dark chocolate. A little white on toes and chest permissible.

Gait: The American Water Spaniel moves with well-balanced reach and drive. Watching a dog move toward one, there should be no signs of elbows being out. Upon viewing the dog from the rear, one should get the impression that the hind legs, which should be well-muscled and not cowhocked, move as nearly parallel as possible, with hocks doing their full share of work and flexing well, thus giving the appearance of power and strength.

Temperament: Demeanor indicates intelligence, eagerness to please and friendly. Great energy and eagerness for the hunt yet controllable in the field.

Disqualification: *Yellow eyes.*

Approved March 13, 1990

Meet the Barbet

Recognized by AKC® in 2020
Barbet Club of America (www.barbetclubofamerica.com), formed in 2009

Traits
- Joyful
- Sweet-Natured
- Bright

HISTORY

The Barbet, also known as the "French Water Dog," developed in France and was once a popular hunting companion to the wealthy and working class alike. The breed was renowned for its work ethic and willingness to flush game and retrieve from the water in any weather conditions. The Barbet is said to have contributed to the lineage of many other water and working dogs, including the Poodle, Otterhound, Newfoundland, and Briard, as well as to that of the Bichon Frise, a favorite companion breed.

The first written mentions of the breed appear in the sixteenth century, and Henry IV, King of France from 1589 to 1610, enjoyed waterfowling with his Barbets. The breed was also depicted in numerous works of art. Because its curly coat forms a beard, the breed's name comes from the French word for "beard"—*barbe*.

The first breed standard for the Barbet was published in 1894. World Wars I and II all but decimated the breed's population, but a small and dedicated following brought the Barbet back from the brink of extinction.

FORM AND FUNCTION

The Barbet possesses essential characteristics of a water dog: the webbed feet aid in swimming, and the breed's signature thick, curly coat protects the dog from the elements, enabling him to retrieve from even the coldest of water. This is a medium-sized dog, slightly longer than tall, with a balanced, athletic build that allows him to perform his duties in the field. He is seen in solid black, gray, brown, fawn as well as in these colors with white markings. In the pied coloration, the dog is primarily white with markings of black, gray, brown, and fawn.

LIVING WITH A BARBET

The Barbet is a talented water dog who can't resist getting his paws wet—or dirty—earning the breed the nickname "mud dog," and he enjoys the water all year round. Barbet fanciers agree that this is an intelligent and joyful dog that learns quickly and makes a calm companion as long as he gets enough activity. Barbet typically get along with people of all ages as well as other dogs when properly socialized.

The nonshedding coat grows continuously and requires regular brushing and trimming to keep it mat-free and at a manageable length.

COMPETITION

The Barbet earned full AKC® recognition in 2020, and can compete in conformation events as well as many of the events offered by the AKC® and its affiliated clubs each year. The breed was approved to compete in AKC® companion events in 2010 and in Retriever Hunting Tests in 2012. With his trainability and athleticism, the Barbet fares well in events such as obedience and agility.

Official Standard for the Barbet

General Appearance: An archetypic water dog of France, the Barbet is a rustic breed of medium size and balanced proportions which appears in works as early as the sixteenth century. In profile, the Barbet is slightly rectangular with a substantial head and long, sweeping tail. He has a long, dense covering of curly hair and a distinctive beard (French *barbe*), which gives the breed its name. An agile athlete, the Barbet has been used primarily to locate, flush, and retrieve birds. He has a cheerful disposition; very social and loyal.

Size, Proportion, Substance: Height at the withers: Dogs 21 to 24½ inches, Bitches 19 to 22½ inches. Weight in proportion to height. *Proportions*—Measured from point of shoulder to buttocks and withers to ground, the Barbet is slightly longer than tall. Exact proportion is not as important as balance. *Substance*—Neither coarse nor refined, the Barbet is solidly built with adequate bone to perform his tasks as a true sporting dog.

Head: Of great importance, the *head* is strong, broad, and proportionally large. *Expression* is bright,

engaging. *Eyes* of medium size, nearly round in shape, dark hazel to dark brown, harmonizing with the coat color. Eye rims are fully pigmented, corresponding to coat (black for black, black pied or gray dogs; brown for brown or brown pied dogs. Fawn dogs may have either black or brown pigmentation). *Ears* are wide and are set at eye level. Ear leather reaching at least to the corner of the mouth and fully covered with long hair. *Skull* is rounded and broad. *Occiput* is not prominent. Stop is defined, neither abrupt nor sloping. Head planes are nearly parallel. The muzzle is shorter than the skull and is quite square. Bridge of nose is broad. Lower jaw fairly square and strong. Jaws of equal length. The nose is large, with well opened nostrils, fully pigmented in harmony with coat color. Lips are thick, fully pigmented. Flews are tight. *Scissors bite*, teeth large and strong.

Neck, Topline and Body: *Neck* is strong, blending well into the body. Back is solid with well sustained level topline, loin is short and slightly arched, croup rounded. *The tail is the natural extension of the* topline, long and low set. When in motion the tail is carried above horizontal in a sweeping curve but does not curl onto the back. The tail is never docked. *Body is athletic with substance,* chest is broad, well-developed, deep, reaching the elbow; ribs rounded but not barrel-like, underline slightly inclined without tuck-up.

Forequarters: Emphasis is on balance. Shoulders are well laid back and approximately the same length as the upper arm, placing the front legs well under the chest with elbows close to the body. Legs are straight and strong; well boned. Pasterns are strong and flexible. Front dewclaws may be removed. Feet are round, and toes are tight, well-arched. Pads thick.

Hindquarters: Angulation balances with forequarters. Upper thigh is well muscled, stifle well bent, second thigh is well developed, hocks well let-down, short and perpendicular to ground; without dewclaws. Feet same as front.

Coat: The coat of the Barbet is his defining characteristic. Profuse hair covers the whole body evenly with thick, natural curls that range from large and loose to tight, smaller curls. The hair on the top of the head reaches the bridge of the nose. He has a distinctive beard. Ears are covered in long hair. The coat is shown in as natural a state as possible; clean and free from mats. The hair is to retain curl. While scissoring is necessary to keep him neat, excessive sculpting and shaping is to be penalized.

Color: All shades of black, gray, brown, fawn; with or without white markings. Pied (primarily white with all shades of black, gray, brown, fawn markings).

Gait: Easy, ground-covering trot with good front reach and impulsion from hindquarters with precise cadence. Feet converge toward the centerline with increased speed. Topline remains level and carriage is smart.

Temperament: The Barbet is a responsive, loving member of the family. Joyful, bright, and kindly natured, he is a versatile sporting dog and willing participant in many activities. The sensitive Barbet responds to positive interaction and training, and displays an even temperament.

Approved December 9, 2015
Effective January 1, 2017

Meet the Boykin Spaniel

Recognized by AKC® in 2009
Boykin Spaniel Club and Breeders Association of America (theboykinspanielclub.com), formed in 1997

Traits
- Fiercely Loyal
- Tenacious
- Assertive

HISTORY

Created by South Carolina hunters, the small, sturdy, cheerful Boykin Spaniel now beautifully adapts to the dove fields, the duck marshes, and anywhere upland birds populate. Early in the twentieth century, Alexander L. White found a small dog wandering near a church in Spartanburg, South Carolina. The dog, soon to be named Dumpy, displayed talent in hunting and retrieving, so White sent him to his hunting partner, L. Whitaker Boykin, near Camden, South Carolina.

Whit Boykin provided dogs to vacationers to hunt the Wateree River swamp areas using *section boats*, small, narrow, flat-bottomed crafts. The Boykin Spaniel soon developed into a superb turkey dog and waterfowl retriever and became known as "the dog who doesn't rock the boat." Boykins became wildly popular among South Carolina's hunters and for decades were relatively unknown outside the area. Other breeds that contributed to the development of the Boykin may include the Chesapeake Bay Retriever and a variety of spaniels.

A true regional treasure, the Boykin Spaniel became South Carolina's official state dog in 1985, and now more Boykins can be found in other states than in South Carolina.

FORM AND FUNCTION

Amazingly versatile, these compact, all-around hunting companions are built for activity and endurance, in both heavy cover and water. Their small size—males 15½ to 18 inches at the shoulder and females 14 to 16½ inches—makes it easy for hunters to lift both dog and duck into a boat after a retrieve. The breed's gait should suggest efficiency and endurance, moving with an air of high spirits and controlled energy.

LIVING WITH A BOYKIN SPANIEL

The Boykin Spaniel is an amazingly versatile and compact gun dog—tenacious, assertive, and enthusiastic both flushing and retrieving, yet gentle and affectionate at home. In the field, Boykin Spaniels steal the show. At home, Boykins capture hearts. Fiercely attached to their owners, they are remarkable companion gun dogs for all seasons.

A loving, affectionate, and fiercely loyal personality is the hallmark of this breed, and Boykins are exquisite family pets. The breed thrives on companionship, enjoying the company of children and other dogs. Boykins are happy to hunt doves all day and then come home and nestle next to you on the couch all evening. As hunting dogs, they have moderate to high energy and do best with active people, especially those seeking companions for sports.

The Boykin Spaniel's medium-length wavy coat—colored in solid rich liver, brown, or dark chocolate possibly with a small amount of white on the chest—requires only minimal maintenance beyond occasional brushing to prevent mats from forming. They are eager, quick to learn, and will benefit from positive and consistent training. Boykins may retain puppylike traits throughout their life.

COMPETITION

Boykin owners say that their dogs are "born ready for anything you want to teach them." Terrific hunting companions, they can participate in AKC® conformation, spaniel hunting tests, and all companion events.

Official Standard for the Boykin Spaniel

General Appearance: The Boykin Spaniel was developed in South Carolina, USA as a medium-sized sporting dog with a docked tail. The breed is built to cover all types of ground conditions with agility and reasonable speed. Size and weight were essential in development of the breed as these hunting companions needed to be lighter and smaller than their larger sporting dog cousins to fit in the portable section boats of the time period. As a result, the Boykin Spaniel came to be known as "the little brown dog that doesn't rock the boat". Being a hunting dog, he should be exhibited in hard muscled working condition. His coat should not be so excessive as to hinder his work as an active flushing spaniel, but should be thick enough to protect him from heavy cover and weather. The Boykin Spaniel is primarily a working gun dog; structure and soundness are of great importance.

Size, Proportion, Substance: The Boykin Spaniel is solidly built, with moderate bone, and smooth firm muscles. The ideal *height* measured from the ground to the highest point of the shoulder blades for dogs is 15½ to 18 inches at the withers; for bitches is 14 to 16½ inches at the withers. Any variance greater than 1 inch above or below the ideal height is a major fault. The minimum height ranges shall not apply to dogs or bitches under 12 months of age. *Proportion* is slightly longer than tall, never square. However, exact proportion is not as important as the dog being well-balanced and sound, capable of performing the breed's intended function.

Head: The *head* must be in proportion with the size of the dog. The *expression* is alert, eager, self-confident, attractive and intelligent. *Eyes* range from yellow to amber to varying shades of brown, set well apart, medium size and almond or oval shaped, and trusting. Protruding or bulging eyes is a major fault. *Ears* are pendulous and set slightly above or even with the line of the eye; ear set is higher when alert. The leather of the ear is thin and when pulled forward should almost reach the tip of the nose. The

AKC Official Guide to Sporting Dogs

ears hang close to the cheeks and are flat. *Skull* is fairly broad, flat on top, and slightly rounded at the sides and back. The occiput bone is inconspicuous. The stop is moderate. When viewed from the side the nasal bone and the top of the skull form two parallel lines. *Muzzle* is approximately the same length as the skull, and is approximately ½ the width of the skull. The distance from the tip of the nose to the occiput is about the same length as occiput to the base of the neck. The nasal bone is straight with no inclination down or of snippiness. The nose is to be fully pigmented, dark liver in color with well opened nostrils. The lips are close fitting and clean, without excess skin or flews. Scissors is the preferred *bite*, level is acceptable. Pronounced or extreme overshot or undershot bites are major faults. Broken teeth should not count against the dog.

Neck, Topline, Body: *Neck* is moderately long, muscular, slightly arched at the crest and gradually blends into sloping shoulders and never concave or ewe-necked. Back—The *topline* is straight, strong and essentially level and should remain solid and level in movement. Loins are short, strong with a slight tuck up. His *body* is sturdily constructed but not too compact and never square. The shoulders are sloping. The brisket is well developed but not barreled, extending to the elbow and not too broad or narrow as to interfere with movement. A $\tfrac{2}{3}$ to $\tfrac{1}{3}$ ribs to loin ratio is preferred. The croup slopes gently to the set of the tail, and the tail-set follows the natural line of the croup. The *tail* is docked to a length of 3 to 5 inches when fully mature. The tail's carriage should be carried horizontally or slightly elevated and displays a characteristic lively, merry action, particularly when the dog is on game.

Forequarters: The Boykin Spaniel's shoulders are sloping, clean and muscular. His legs medium in length, straight and well boned but not too short as to handicap for field work or so heavy as to appear clumsy. Pasterns are strong with no suggestion of weakness. Feet are round, compact, well-arched, of medium size with thick pads. Dewclaws should be removed. The toes closely grouped, webbed and well padded.

Hindquarters: The Boykin Spaniel has well developed hips and thighs with moderate angulation at the stifle with the whole rear assembly showing strength and drive. Hindquarters are muscular and most importantly, in balance with

the forequarters. Hocks well let down, pasterns relatively short, strong and parallel when viewed from the rear. Feet—see feet under forequarters.

Coat: The coat can range from flat to slightly wavy to curly, with medium length. The Boykin Spaniel is typically a single coat breed but may have undercoat. Boykin Spaniels are considered a "wash and wear" dog easily going from the field to the ring. The ears, chest, legs and belly are equipped with light fringe or feathering. His coat may be trimmed, never shaved, to have a well-groomed appearance and to enhance the dog's natural lines. It is legitimate to trim about the head, throat, ears, tail and feet to give a smart, functional but natural appearance. Honorable field scars are acceptable.

Color: The Boykin Spaniel color is a solid liver color—a deep reddish brown color that includes various shades of chocolate brown, from light to very dark. A small amount of white on the chest is permitted and no other white markings are allowed. Sun bleaching is acceptable.

Gait: Movement is effortless with good reach from well laidback shoulders at an angle that permits a long stride that is in balance with the rear quarters for strong driving power with no wasted movement. Viewed from the rear the hocks should drive well under the body following on a line with the forelegs neither too widely nor closely spaced. As speed increases it is natural for the legs to fall to a center line of travel. Seen from the side it should exhibit a good, long forward stride with no side winding. In gait the tail is carried level to or above the back.

Temperament: The Boykin Spaniel is friendly, a willing worker, intelligent and easy to train. The Boykin Spaniel thrives on human companionship and gets along well with other dogs and children. He shows great eagerness and energy for the hunt yet controllable in the field.

Faults: The foregoing description is that of the ideal Boykin Spaniel. Any deviation from the above described dog must be penalized to the extent of the deviation.

Approved January 8, 2019
Effective April 2, 2019

Meet the Bracco Italiano

Recognized by AKC® in 2022
Bracco Italiano Club of America (thebraccoclub.org) founded in 2007

Traits
- Driven
- Sweet
- Intelligent

HISTORY

The flashy, fast trotting Bracco Italiano is among the oldest of the European pointers, with a history that breed experts say dates back to the fourth and fifth centuries B.C. The breed may have descended from Segugio Italiano, a coursing hound, and molossers, or ancient mastiffs.

By the Middle Ages, the Bracco was considered a distinct breed in Italy. During the Renaissance, they were favored by aristocracy, and hunted alongside members of the powerful Medici and Gonzaga families.

Originally, Bracchi Italiani were used to drive quarry into nets or to flush birds for falconers. With the emergence of firearms, the Bracco developed gun dog skills—hunt, point, and retrieve. Along with the Spinone Italiano, the breed is one of two gun dogs native to Italy.

By the end of the 19th century, the Bracco Italiano was facing extinction. An Italian fancier, Ferdinand Delour de Ferrabouc (1838–1913), is credited with leading the efforts to bring them back from the brink.

At one time, there were two varieties that had emerged in different parts of Italy—the Piedmontese and Lombard pointers. In the 1920s these varieties merged. The Italian standard was released in 1949.

Bracchi Italiani first came to the United States in the 1990s. They were accepted into the AKC® Foundation Stock Service® in 2001. In 2022, the Bracco Italiano became the 200th AKC®-recognized breed, entering the Sporting Group. They are still rare beyond the borders of Italy, with only about 600 to 700 in the United States at the time of AKC® recognition.

FORM AND FUNCTION

A Bracco Italiano working in the field is a breathtaking sight, thanks in part to a distinctive gait known as the extended or flying trot. This smooth movement, a hallmark of the breed, is fast and so efficient the dogs seem to be gliding. As air-scenters, they hold their heads higher than their toplines, as if they are being "pulled along by the nose." That nose, the breed standard notes, should be "voluminous, with large well-opened nostrils," well-designed to detect a scent trail.

They are large and solidly built, with the preferred height at the withers of 21 to 27 inches. Their powerful legs and large feet serve them well on land and in water; Bracchi Italiani are excellent swimmers.

They come in a variety of colors, including white, bright orange and white, and soft brown and white.

LIVING WITH A BRACCO ITALIANO

Some US owners became aware of the Bracco Italiano by stumbling across a picture in a book or on the web. They were attracted by the long ears, wrinkles, and skin folds that give them their hound-dog expression. In public, Bracco owners often find themselves answering questions like, "Where did you get a Basset Hound with such long legs?" or "Is that a Bloodhound mixed with a Pointer?"

In the field, the Bracco Italiano is driven, serious, all-business. But at home, most owners say it's like they flip a switch into domestic mode—loving, sweet, and sometimes goofy.

If they are given adequate exercise for body and mind, they are happy to drape themselves on the couch or share a nap with you. Some have the retriever trait of wanting to carry things in their mouths and will often greet you at the door with a present, like your shoe or a toy. They are moderate shedders and tend to drool a bit.

Words used to describe their unique temperament are thoughtful, intelligent, and family-oriented. The Bracco Italiano needs to be included in the household activities, and they learn quickly and best with gentle, clear training.

COMPETITION

The Bracco Italiano is first and foremost a hunting dog; it is in their blood. They excel in field trials and hunting. They are also eligible to compete in other events, including AKC® conformation, agility, obedience, rally, Scent Work, and Barn Hunt.

Official Standard for the Bracco Italiano

General Appearance: Of strong and harmonious construction, powerful appearance. The preferred subjects are smooth coated, with lean limbs, well-developed muscles, well defined lines, and a markedly sculpted head with very obvious chiseling under the eyes. These elements all contribute to give distinction to this breed. The Bracco is tough and adapted to all types of hunting, reliable, docile, and easy to train.

Size, Proportion, Substance: Height at the withers between 21 to 27 inches. Preferred size for males: 23 to 27 inches; preferred size for females: 21 to 25 inches. Weight between 55 to 90 pounds, depending on height. Height at the withers less than 21 inches after 12 months of age is a disqualification. Height greater than 27 inches is a disqualification. The Bracco is a solidly built dog with powerful bone, but without lumber, and without sacrificing balance and harmonious appearance. A dog in hard and lean field condition is not to be penalized. Important *Proportions*: The body is square or slightly longer than tall. Length of head is equal to two-fifths (40 percent) of the height at the withers; its width, measured at the level of the zygomatic arches, is less than half its length. Skull and muzzle are of equal length.

Head: *Head*—Angular and narrow at the level of the zygomatic arches, its length corresponds to two-fifths (40 percent) of the height at the withers; the middle of its length is at the level of a line that unites the inner angles of both eyes. The upper planes of the skull and muzzle are divergent, i.e.: if extended, the top line of the muzzle emerges in front of the occiput, ideally at mid-length of the skull (down-faced). Dish face (convergence of the planes of the skull and muzzle) is a disqualification. The head and neck are moderate in skin. The head should have a soft fold of skin from the outer corner of the eye, falling down the cheek. When the head is down and relaxed, there is a skin fold across the skull from ear to ear. *Eyes*—Semi-lateral position, neither deep set nor prominent. Eyes fairly large, eyelids oval-shaped and close-fitting (no entropion or ectropion). The iris is a dark amber to orange or brown color depending

on the color of the coat. Wall eye is a disqualification. Expression is soft, gentle and intelligent. *Ears*—Well developed. In length they should, without being stretched, reach the tip of the nose. Their width is at least equal to half their length; raised only very slightly; base rather narrow, set at level of zygomatic arches. A supple ear with a front rim well-turned inwards to frame the face; the lower extremity of the ear ends in a slightly rounded tip. *Skull* Region: Seen in profile, the skull shape is a very open arch. Seen from the top, it forms lengthwise an elongated oval. The width of the skull measured at the level of the zygomatic arches should not exceed half the length of the head. Cheeks are lean, the bulge of the forehead and the supra-orbital ridges are perceptible. The stop is not pronounced. The frontal groove is visible and ends at mid-length of the skull. The interparietal crest is short and not very prominent. The occiput is pronounced. *Muzzle*—Fore-face is either straight or slightly arched. Its length is equal to half of the length of the head and its depth measures four-fifths (80 percent) of its length. Seen from the front, the lateral sides of the muzzle converge slightly, still presenting a fore-face of good width. The chin is not very apparent. *Nose*—Voluminous, with large well-opened nostrils, protrudes slightly over the lips with which it forms an angle. Color brown or from pale pink to more or less deep fleshy red depending on the color of the coat. A split nose is a disqualification. *Lips*—Upper lips well developed, thin and floppy without being flaccid, covering the jaw; seen in profile, they overlap the lower jaw slightly, seen from the front, they form an inverted "V" below the nose; the corner of the lips must be marked without being droopy. *Teeth*—Dental arches well adapted, with the teeth square to the jaw. *Bite*—Scissor or level. Any deviation (overbite or underbite) should be faulted in accordance to its severity.

Neck, Topline, Body: *Neck*—Powerful, in truncated cone shape. Length of the neck is at least two-thirds but not greater than the length of the head. Well detached from the nape. The throat shows a soft double dewlap. Excessive skin with exaggerated wrinkling or single dewlap is faulted. *Topline*—The upper profile of the back is made up of two lines: one, almost straight, slopes from the withers to the 11th dorsal vertebrae (mid-back); the other is slightly arched, joining with the line of the croup. *Body*—Chest is broad, deep and well down to level of the elbows, without forming a keel. Ribs well sprung, particularly in their lower part, and sloping. Wide lumbar region. Loin is well muscled, short and slightly convex. Croup is long (about one-third of the height at the withers), wide and well-muscled; the pelvic angulation (angle formed by the pelvic girdle with a horizontal line) is 30 degrees. *Underline*—Lower profile almost horizontal in its rib cage part, rising slightly in its abdominal part. *Tail*—Thick at the base, straight, with a slight tendency to taper, hair short. When the dog is in action and especially when questing, is carried horizontally or nearly. *Docked*—Should be docked 6 to 10 inches from the root. *Undocked*—Carried horizontally; length of the undocked tail is to the hock. May be slightly curved but never held high or carried bent over the back.

Forequarters: Withers are well defined, with the points of the shoulder blades well separated. Shoulder strong, well-muscled, long, sloping, and well laid back, very free in its movement. The upper arm sloping, fitting to the rib cage. Forearm strong, straight, with well-marked sinews; the point of the elbows should be on a perpendicular line from the rear point of the shoulder blade to the ground. Metacarpus (pastern) well proportioned, lean, of good length and slightly sloping. Feet strong, slightly oval shaped, well arched and closed toes with strong nails well curved towards the ground. Color of nails is white, yellow or brown, of a more or less dark shade depending on the color of the coat. Foot pads elastic and lean.

Hindquarters: In balance with the forequarters. Thigh long, parallel, muscular, with the rear edge almost straight when viewed from the side. Strong limbs; hocks wide, metatarsals (rear pasterns) relatively short and lean. The feet, with all the characteristics of the front feet, have dewclaws, the absence of which is not a fault. Double dewclaws are tolerated.

Coat: *Skin*—Ample skin, tough but elastic, well separated from the tissues underneath; fine on the head, the throat, inside the elbows, and on lower part of the body. The visible mucous membranes must be a corresponding color with the coat, but never show black spots. The mucous membranes of the mouth are pink; sometimes with light brown spotting.
Coat—Short, dense and glossy, fine and shorter on the head, the ears, front part of the legs and feet.

Color: The base color is white. The colors acceptable in this breed are: solid white, white with orange markings, or white with brown markings. The markings are of varied sizes (patches, ticking, or roan). A symmetrical face mask is preferred, but the absence of a mask is tolerated. The orange color can range from a dark amber to rich orange. It is not lemon or yellow. The brown color is a warm shade that recalls the color of a monk's frock (Crayola Brown); it is not liver. A metallic sheen is appreciated in brown and white dogs. Disqualifying colors—Tricolor, or with tan markings, fawn, hazel. Any trace of black on coat or mucous membranes. Any solid color other than white. Albinism.

Gait: Extended and fast trot, with powerful reach and drive. Head raised, nose held high in such a way that, when hunting, the nose is higher than the topline as if the dog is being "pulled along by the nose." The fluid, powerful, and extended trot is hallmark of this breed.

Temperament: The Bracco is tough and adapted to all types of hunting, reliable, docile, and intelligent. Friendly, not shy, never aggressive, and readily makes eye contact. Extreme shyness is a fault. Aggressiveness is a disqualification.

Fault: Any departure from the foregoing constitutes a fault which when judging must be penalized according to its seriousness and its extension.

Disqualifications: *Height at the withers less than 21 inches after 12 months of age. Height greater than 27 inches. Dish face (convergence of the planes of the skull and muzzle). Wall eye. Split nose. Tricolor, tan markings, fawn or hazel color. Any trace of black on coat or mucous membranes. Any solid color other than white. Albinism. Aggressiveness.*

Approved October 8, 2018
Effective July 3, 2019

AKC Official Guide to Sporting Dogs

Meet the Brittany

Recognized by AKC® in 1934
as the "Brittany Spaniel"; official name changed to "Brittany" in 1982 American Brittany Club (theamericanbrittanyclub.org), formed in 1942

Traits
- Energetic
- Bright
- Sense of Humor

HISTORY

French peasants in the area known as Bretagne developed this "spaniel"-type dog (a mixture of spaniel and pointer) to poach on their landlord's property. The dogs would point and then drop to the ground while their owner threw a net over the game in front of them. The Brittany also earned his keep as a family dog, watchdog, and general hunting dog. The climate, nature of terrain to be hunted, and the manner of hunting had their effect on the breed's size, coat, keen nose, and retrieving ability. The first record of the importation of Brittanys into the United States was in 1912. More were imported in 1928, but most came here in the 1930s, and these dogs became the foundation of today's Brittany on American soil.

FORM AND FUNCTION

The Brittany standard was written to maintain the hunting function of the breed, with such features as well open nostrils to permit deep breathing and adequate scenting, chest deep and reaching to the elbow, ribs well sprung, and lips tight and dry, so that feathers will not stick. Due to the vigilance of breeders, Brittanys have more dual champions than any other sporting breed. The Brittany may be lacking a tail, or have one approximately 4 inches in length, natural or docked. Since Brittanys hunt in thorny cover, a long tail opens the risk of infection.

LIVING WITH A BRITTANY

In selecting a puppy, a prospective buyer must realize that this is an active breed that needs exercise. While apartment living is not ideal, a dedicated owner can provide adequate exercise and mental stimulation to channel the dog's abundant energy. Due to the breed's intelligence, basic obedience is recommended. Gentle and consistent training is the key. Brittanys are "people" dogs who love attention and have a distinct sense of humor. Their coat sheds dirt and mud when allowed to dry and requires a brushing once or twice a week. With proper nutrition and exercise, most Brittanys live twelve to fourteen years. If you are an outdoorsy type looking for a similar companion, you might be worthy of this energetic hunter.

COMPETITION

Brittanys are extremely versatile and want to please. They compete in pointing breed field trials, hunting tests, conformation, obedience, agility, flyball, lure coursing, and tracking. They also take part, when properly trained, in therapy work, visiting nursing homes, rehab facilities, and hospitals.

Official Standard for the Brittany

General Appearance: A compact, closely knit dog of medium size, a leggy dog having the appearance, as well as the agility, of a great ground coverer. Strong, vigorous, energetic and quick of movement. Ruggedness, without clumsiness, is a characteristic of the breed. He can be tailless or has a tail docked to approximately 4 inches.

Size, Proportion, Substance: *Height*—17½ to 20½ inches, measured from the ground to the highest point of the shoulders. Any Brittany measuring under 17½ inches or over 20½ inches shall be disqualified from dog show competition. *Weight*—Should weigh between 30 and 40 pounds. *Proportion*—So leggy is he that his height at the shoulders is the same as the length of his body. *Body Length*—Approximately the same as the height when measured at the shoulders. Body length is measured from the point of the forechest to the rear of the rump. A long body should be heavily penalized. *Substance*—Not too light in bone, yet never heavy-boned and cumbersome.

Head: *Expression*—Alert and eager, but with the soft expression of a bird dog. *Eyes*—Well set in head. Well protected from briars by a heavy, expressive eyebrow. A prominent full or popeye should be penalized. It is a serious fault in a dog that must face briars. Skull well chiseled under the eyes, so that the lower lid is not pulled back to form a pocket or haw that would catch seeds, dirt and weed dust. Preference should be for the darker colored eyes, though lighter shades of amber should not be penalized. Light and mean-looking eyes should be heavily penalized. *Ears*—Set high, above the level of the eyes. Short and triangular, rather than pendulous, reaching about half the length of the muzzle. Should lie flat and close to the head, with dense, but relatively short hair, and with little fringe. *Skull*—Medium length, rounded, very slightly wedge-shaped, but evenly made. Width, not quite as wide as the length and never so broad as to appear coarse, or so narrow as to appear racy. Well defined, but gently sloping stop. Median line rather indistinct. The occiput only apparent to the touch. Lateral walls well rounded. The Brittany should never be "apple-headed" and he should never have an indented stop. *Muzzle*—Medium length, about two-thirds the length of the skull, measuring the muzzle from the tip to the stop, and the skull from the occiput to the stop. Muzzle should taper gradually in both horizontal and vertical dimensions as it approaches the nostrils. Neither a Roman nose nor a dish-face is desirable. Never broad, heavy or snipy. *Nose*—Nostrils well open to permit deep breathing of air and adequate scenting. Tight nostrils should be penalized. Never shiny. *Color:* fawn, tan, shades of brown or deep pink. A black nose is a disqualification. A two-tone or butterfly nose should be penalized. *Lips*—Tight, the upper lip overlapping the lower jaw just to cover the lower lip. Lips dry, so that feathers will not stick. Drooling to be heavily penalized. Flews to be penalized. *Bite*—A true scissors bite. Overshot or undershot jaw to be heavily penalized.

Neck, Topline, Body: *Neck*—Medium length. Free from throatiness, though not a serious fault unless accompanied by dewlaps, strong without giving the impression of being over muscled. Well set into sloping shoulders. Never concave or ewe-necked. *Topline*—Slight slope from the highest point of the shoulders to the root of the tail. *Chest*—Deep, reaching the level of the elbow. Neither so wide nor so rounded as to disturb the placement of the shoulders and elbows. Ribs well sprung. Adequate heart room provided by depth as well as width. Narrow or slab-sided chests are a fault. *Back*—Short and straight. Never hollow, saddle, sway or roach backed. Slight drop from the hips to the root of the tail. *Flanks*—Rounded. Fairly full. Not extremely tucked up, or flabby and falling. Loins short and strong. Distance from last rib to upper thigh short, about three to four finger widths. Narrow and weak loins are a fault. In motion, the loin should not sway sideways, giving a zig-zag motion to the back, wasting energy. *Tail*—Tailless to approximately 4 inches, natural or docked. The tail not to be so long as to affect the overall balance of the dog. Set on high, actually an extension of the spine at about the same level. Any tail substantially more than 4 inches shall be severely penalized.

Forequarters: *Shoulders*—Shoulder blades should not protrude too much, not too wide apart, with perhaps two thumbs' width between. Sloping and muscular. Blade and upper arm should form nearly a 90-degree angle. Straight shoulders are a fault. At the shoulders, the Brittany is slightly higher than at the rump. *Front legs*—Viewed from the front, perpendicular, but not set too wide. Elbows and feet turning neither in nor out. Pasterns slightly sloped. Down in pasterns is a serious fault. Leg bones clean, graceful, but not too fine. Extremely heavy bone is as much a fault as spindly legs. One must look for substance and suppleness. Height at elbows should approximately equal distance from elbow to withers. *Feet*—Should be strong, proportionately smaller than the spaniels', with close fitting, well arched toes and thick pads. The Brittany is "not up on his toes." Toes not heavily feathered. Flat feet, splayed

feet, paper feet, etc., are to be heavily penalized. An ideal foot is halfway between the hare and the cat foot. Dewclaws may be removed.

Hindquarters: Broad, strong and muscular, with powerful thighs and well bent stifles, giving the angulation necessary for powerful drive. *Hind legs*—Stifles well bent. The stifle should not be so angulated as to place the hock joint far out behind the dog. A Brittany should not be condemned for straight stifle until the judge has checked the dog in motion from the side. The stifle joint should not turn out making a cowhock. Thighs well feathered but not profusely, halfway to the hock. Hocks, that is, the back pasterns, should be moderately short, pointing neither in nor out, perpendicular when viewed from the side. They should be firm when shaken by the judge. *Feet*—Same as front feet.

Coat: Dense, flat or wavy, never curly. Texture neither wiry nor silky. Ears should carry little fringe. The front and hind legs should have some feathering, but too little is definitely preferable to too much. Dogs with long or profuse feathering or furnishings shall be so severely penalized as to effectively eliminate them from competition. *Skin*—Fine and fairly loose. A loose skin rolls with briars and sticks, thus diminishing punctures or tearing. A skin so loose as to form pouches is undesirable.

Color: Orange and white or liver and white in either clear or roan patterns. Some ticking is desirable. The orange or liver is found in the standard parti-color or piebald patterns. Washed out colors are not desirable. Tri-colors are allowed but not preferred. A tri-color is a liver and white dog with classic orange markings on eyebrows, muzzle and cheeks, inside the ears and under the tail; freckles on the lower legs are orange. Anything exceeding the limits of these markings shall be severely penalized. Black is a disqualification.

Gait: When at a trot the Brittany's hind foot should step into or beyond the print left by the front foot. Clean movement, coming and going, is very important, but most important is side gait, which is smooth, efficient and ground covering.

Temperament: A happy, alert dog, neither mean nor shy.

Disqualifications: *Any Brittany measuring under 17½ inches or over 20½ inches. A black nose. Black in the coat.*

Approved April 10, 1990
Effective May 31, 1990

Meet the Chesapeake Bay Retriever

Recognized by AKC® in 1878
American Chesapeake Club (amchessieclub.org), formed in 1918

Traits
- Intelligent
- Courageous
- Sensitive

HISTORY

In the 1800s, duck clubs lined the Chesapeake Bay and shot thousands of birds in a season for the markets of the large Eastern cities. A truly American sporting breed and the toughest of water retrievers, the Chesapeake Bay Retriever was developed along the eastern shore of Maryland to hunt these waterfowl under the most adverse weather and water conditions. The origins of the breed are said to stem from two Newfoundland dogs (Sailor and Canton) rescued from a brig sinking in the Chesapeake Bay in 1807. Using Sailor and Canton's descendants, along with infusions of various hounds and Irish Water Spaniels, the clubs developed the breed known today as the Chesapeake Bay Retriever. Selection was based on working attributes of love of water, thick coat, conformation for swimming, birdiness, strength, intelligence, and perseverance. The dogs were expected to figure out problems, be protective but not aggressive of their masters' birds and blind, and be devoted to their families.

FORM AND FUNCTION

The Chesapeake's signature traits enable him to work: a water-resistant double coat that has a thick wooly undercoat for protection against the cold and a coarse and wavy outer coat; a body that is strong and muscular with a broad deep chest, well-laid shoulders, a powerful rear with well-webbed large hare feet for swimming; a head that has small ears held high as to be out of the water and a pointed but not sharp muzzle shape with length to hold game birds easily. While a superb waterfowl dog, the breed is a versatile hunter equally suited to working upland game birds. The Chessie comes in three colors—brown, sedge (red), and deadgrass (blonde)—all of which are equally preferred. The breed remains today a valued hunter and beloved companion that participates in many AKC® events.

LIVING WITH A CHESSIE

This is not a breed for everyone because Chessies require their owners to be in control. Chessies are intelligent and "thinking" dogs with exceptional memories. Once they learn something, it really stays with them—good or bad. Training should start in puppyhood with obedience classes. Socialization is a must for this breed that is ideally suited to owners who enjoy outdoor activities, want a close relationship with their dog, and who are committed to working with their dog. Exercise needs are moderate. Chessies love swimming, hiking, boating, and almost anything as long as they are with their owner. They are calm and sensible dogs in the house and have more watchdog instincts than other retrieving breeds.

COMPETITION

The breed is eligible to compete in conformation, retriever field trials, hunting tests, and all companion events.

Official Standard for the Chesapeake Bay Retriever

General Appearance: Equally proficient on land and in the water, the Chesapeake Bay Retriever was developed along the Chesapeake Bay to hunt waterfowl under the most adverse weather and water conditions, often having to break ice during the course of many strenuous multiple retrieves. Frequently the Chesapeake must face wind, tide and long cold swims in its work. The breed's characteristics are specifically suited to enable the Chesapeake to function with ease, efficiency and endurance. In head, the Chesapeake's skull is broad and round with a medium stop. The jaws should be of sufficient length and strength to carry large game birds with an easy, tender hold. The double coat consists of a short, harsh, wavy outer coat and a dense, fine, wooly undercoat containing an abundance of natural oil and is ideally suited for the icy rugged conditions of weather the Chesapeake often works in. In body, the Chesapeake is a strong, well-balanced, powerfully built animal of moderate size and medium length in body and leg, deep and wide in chest, the shoulders built with full liberty of movement, and with no tendency to weakness in any feature, particularly the rear. The power, though, should not be at the expense of agility or stamina. Size and substance should not be excessive as this is a working retriever of an active nature.

Distinctive features include eyes that are very clear, of yellowish or amber hue, hindquarters as high or a trifle higher than the shoulders, and a double coat which tends to wave on shoulders, neck, back and loins only.

The Chesapeake is valued for its bright and happy disposition, intelligence, quiet good sense, and affectionate protective nature. Extreme shyness or extreme aggressive tendencies are not desirable in the breed either as a gun dog or companion.

Disqualifications: Specimens that are lacking in breed characteristics should be disqualified.

Size, Proportion, Substance: *Height*—Males should measure 23 to 26 inches; females should measure 21 to 24 inches. *Oversized* or *undersized* animals *are* to be *severely penalized*. *Proportion*—Height from the top of the shoulder blades to the ground should be slightly less than the body length from the breastbone to the point of buttocks. Depth of body should extend at least to the elbow. Shoulder to elbow and elbow to ground should be equal.

Chesapeake Bay Retriever

Weight—Males should weigh 65 to 80 pounds; females should weigh 55 to 70 pounds.

Head: The Chesapeake Bay Retriever should have an intelligent expression. *Eyes* are to be medium large, very clear, of yellowish or amber color and wide apart. *Ears* are to be small, set well up on the head, hanging loosely, and of medium leather. *Skull* is broad and round with a medium stop. *Nose* is medium short. *Muzzle* is approximately the same length as the skull, tapered, pointed but not sharp. *Lips* are thin, not pendulous. *Bite*—Scissors is preferred, but a level bite is acceptable.

Disqualifications: Either undershot or overshot bites are to be disqualified.

Neck, Topline, Body: *Neck* should be of medium length with a strong muscular appearance, tapering to the shoulders. *Topline* should show the hindquarters to be as high as or a trifle higher than the shoulders. *Back* should be short, well coupled and powerful. *Chest* should be strong, deep and wide. Rib cage barrel round and deep. *Body* is of medium length, neither cobby nor roached, but rather approaching hollowness from underneath as the flanks should be well tucked up. *Tail* of medium length; medium heavy at the base. The tail should be straight or slightly curved and should not curl over back or side kink.

Forequarters: There should be no tendency to weakness in the forequarters. *Shoulders* should be sloping with full liberty of action, plenty of power and without any restrictions of movement. *Legs* should be medium in length and straight, showing good bone and muscle. Pasterns slightly bent and of medium length. The front legs should appear straight when viewed from front or rear. Dewclaws on the forelegs may be removed. Well webbed hare feet should be of good size with toes well-rounded and close.

Hindquarters: Good hindquarters are essential. They should show fully as much power as the forequarters. There should be no tendency to weakness in the hindquarters. Hindquarters should be especially powerful to supply the driving power for swimming. Legs should be medium length and straight, showing good bone and muscle. Stifles should be well angulated. The distance from hock to ground should be of medium length. The hind legs should look straight when viewed from the front or rear. Dewclaws, if any, must be removed from the hind legs. **Disqualifications:** Dewclaws on the hind legs are a disqualification.

Coat: Coat should be thick and short, nowhere over 1½ inches long, with a dense fine wooly undercoat. Hair on the face and legs should be very short and straight with a tendency to wave on the shoulders,

in extremely thick undergrowth where game birds are likely to be hiding. Their dense coat protects their body, and their heavy brow protects their eyes. Clumbers are rather slow, methodical workers, remaining well within gun range, and they generally hunt mute. Their white coat makes them easy to see in the field. Clumbers have a keen sense of smell and a soft mouth, which make them ideal for retrieving game.

LIVING WITH A CLUMBER

The Clumber Spaniel is a rare breed with a small gene pool. The Clumber Spaniel Club of America encourages potential puppy buyers to only consider buying a puppy from a reputable breeder who breeds for the improvement of the breed while putting the health concerns of the Clumber Spaniel into their breeding decisions. The Clumber Spaniel is described as dignified, charming, loving, entertaining, inquisitive, affectionate, mischievous, stubborn, determined, self-willed, and naughty. They are good with children and amiable with other animals. They should not be left outside alone day after day. They need and deserve the love, attention, and presence of their owners. Clumbers often drool, and they shed all year. The largest of the spaniel breeds, their size is often underestimated. They are a medium to large dog, with males weighing 70 to 85 pounds and females weighing 55 to 70 pounds. The Clumber Spaniel is highly adaptable to various living situations and is one of the few sporting breeds that can adapt to living in an apartment as long as the dog receives moderate daily exercise. This is not the breed of choice for people who wish to run long distances with their pet. The Clumber Spaniel is readily trained and responds well to positive reinforcement utilizing treats, toys, play, and praise. Harsh training methods are ineffective with this sensitive breed. Clumbers do not require extensive grooming but should be brushed two to three times a week to prevent mats. Trimming the excess hair on their ears, feet, and between their pads is recommended.

COMPETITION

The versatile Clumber Spaniel participates successfully in conformation, spaniel hunting tests, obedience,

rally, tracking, and agility. His keen nose makes him a natural dog for tracking, and his happy disposition and loyalty are beneficial in performance events. Clumbers are enthusiastic workers and enjoy adding their own comical antics to routines to keep them interesting.

Official Standard for the Clumber Spaniel

General Appearance: The Clumber Spaniel is a long, low, substantial dog. His heavy brow, deep chest, straight forelegs, powerful hindquarters, massive bone and good feet all give him the power and endurance to move through dense underbrush in pursuit of game. His white coat enables him to be seen by the hunter as he works within gun range. His stature is dignified, his expression pensive, but at the same time he shows great enthusiasm for work and play.

Size, Proportion, Substance: The Clumber is rectangular in shape possessing massive bone structure and has the appearance of great power. The ideal height for dogs is 18 to 20 inches at the withers and for bitches is 17 to 19 inches at the withers. The ideal length to height is 11 to 9 measured from the withers to the base of the tail and from the floor to the withers. Dogs weigh between 70 and 85 pounds and bitches weigh between 55 and 70 pounds.

Head: The head is massive with a marked stop and heavy brow. The top skull is flat with a pronounced occiput. A slight furrow runs between the eyes and up through the center of the skull. The muzzle is broad and deep to facilitate retrieving many species of game. The nose is large, square and colored shades of brown, which include beige, rose and cherry. The flews of the upper jaw are strongly developed and overlap the lower jaw to give a square look when viewed from the side. A scissors bite is preferred. The eyes are dark amber in color, large, soft in expression, and deep set in either a diamond shaped rim or a rim with a "V" on the bottom and a curve on the top. Some haw may show but excessive haw is undesirable. Prominent or round shaped eyes are to be penalized. Excessive tearing or evidence of entropion or ectropion is to be penalized. Ears are broad on top with thick ear leather. The ears are triangular in shape with a rounded lower edge, set low and attached to the skull at approximately eye level.

Neck, Topline, Body: The Clumber should have a long neck with some slackness of throat or presence of dewlap not to be faulted. The neck is strong and muscular, fitting into a well laid back shoulder. The back is straight, firm, long and level. The brisket is deep and the ribs well sprung. The chest is deep and wide. The loin arches slightly. The tail is well feathered and set on just below the line of back; its trimming minimal, serving to tidy the feathering to allow for a natural appearance and outline. The

tail is normally carried level with the topline or slightly elevated, never down between the rear legs. The tail may be docked or left natural, both being of equal value. If docked, the tail's length should be in keeping with the overall proportion of the adult dog. If natural, the tailbone should extend to the point of hock, but should not extend to the ground.

Forequarters: The Clumber shoulder is well laid back. The upper arm is of sufficient length to place the elbow under the highest point of the shoulder. The forelegs are short, straight and heavy in bone, with elbows held close to the body. Pasterns are strong and only slightly sloped. The front feet are large, compact and have thick pads that act as shock absorbers. Removal of dewclaws is optional.

Hindquarters: The thighs are heavily muscled and, when viewed from behind, the rear is round and broad. The stifle shows good functional angulation, and hock to heel is short and perpendicular to the ground. Lack of angulation is objectionable. The rear feet are not as large or as round as on the front feet but compact, with thick pads and are of substantial size.

Coat: The body coat is dense, straight and flat. It is of good weather resistant texture, which is soft to the touch, not harsh. Ears are slightly feathered with straight hair. Feathering on the legs and belly is moderate. The Clumber has a good neck frill and on no condition should his throat be shaved. Evidence of shaving is to be penalized. The hair on the feet should be trimmed neatly to show their natural outline and for utility in the field. The rear legs may be trimmed up to the point of the hock. Tail feathering may be tidied. Trimming of whiskers is optional.

Color and Markings: The Clumber is primarily a white dog with lemon color or orange color markings. Markings are frequently seen on one or both ears and the face. Facial markings include color around one or both eyes, freckling on the muzzle and a spot on top of the head. A head with lemon/orange markings and an all-white head are of equal value. Freckles on the legs and/or a spot near the root of the tail are also frequently seen and acceptable. The body should have as few markings as possible.

Gait: The Clumber moves easily and freely with good reach in front and strong drive from behind, neither crossing over nor elbowing out. The hocks drive in a straight line without rocking or twisting. Because of his wide body and short legs he tends to roll slightly. The proper Clumber roll occurs when the dog, with the correct proportion, reaches forward with the rear leg toward the centerline of travel and rotates the hip downward while the back remains level and straight. The gait is comfortable and can be maintained at a steady trot for a day of work in the field without exhaustion.

Temperament: The Clumber Spaniel is a gentle, loyal and affectionate dog. He possesses an intrinsic desire to please. An intelligent and independent thinker, he displays determination and a strong sense of purpose while at work. A dog of dignity, the Clumber Spaniel may sometimes seem aloof with people unknown to him, but in time he will display his playful and loving nature. The Clumber Spaniel should never be hostile or aggressive; neither is acceptable and should not be condoned.

Approved January 8, 2001
Effective March 28, 2001

Meet the Cocker Spaniel

Recognized by AKC® in 1878
American Spaniel Club (americanspanielclub.org), formed in 1881

Traits
- Merry
- Charming
- Gentle

HISTORY

The Cocker Spaniel is the smallest of the sporting spaniels. Highly trainable, with stamina and intelligence, Cocker Spaniels are known for their strong attachment to people. Their dark eyes reflect a particular sensitivity to human emotions and behavior.

Today's Cocker Spaniels emerged from a larger spaniel population during the 1800s in England. In the first dog shows organized in England, they were often shown as Field Spaniels; later, they were shown in classes for Other Small Breeds of Spaniels. It was at the Ashton show in 1883 that the first class for Cocker Spaniels was offered. The foundation stock of the breed was shown at these early shows, and, shortly after that time, The Kennel Club established a stud book for Cocker Spaniels. Dogs listed in it could be any color but could not weigh more than 25 pounds. Weight was the sole breed characteristic at the time.

During the late 1800s, the first Cocker Spaniels were imported to North America. Breeders in Canada and the United States imported dogs from the finest lines found in England. The Cocker's North American debut in the show ring was in Massachusetts in 1875. The dogs exhibited were long backed and short legged, and Cockers remained so until the 1930s, when Herman Mellenthin's iconic sire, Red Brucie, produced a more up-on-leg dog with a shorter back, the type seen today. Another one of Mellenthin's dogs, My Own Brucie, was one of the most successful show dogs in the breed and propelled Cocker Spaniels to the top of the breed popularity charts. Merry, happy, and affectionate, today's Cocker Spaniel is versatile and competes at the highest levels in agility and flyball events, as well as doing community-service work in animal-assisted therapy programs.

Spaniels of many kinds have held the hearts of people for hundreds of years, but the Cocker Spaniel with his intelligent, gentle nature, and impish playfulness continues to enchant and delight those who experience the depths reflected in those wonderful Cocker Spaniel eyes.

FORM AND FUNCTION

At 14 to 15 inches at the shoulder, Cocker Spaniels are the smallest of the sporting spaniels. They work close to the hunter to find, flush, and retrieve game birds. Using their keen sense of smell, they burrow into thick brush and thickets often too compact for larger spaniel breeds. They are agile workers in hedgerows but will also work in open prairies and woods. Cockers are capable swimmers and will retrieve game from water. They are shown in conformation in three acceptable colors: Black, ASCOB (Any Solid Color Other than Black), and Parti-color, white in combination with other solid colors.

LIVING WITH A COCKER

The Cocker Spaniel is a merry, happy, can-do dog, and he will be a charming companion for all kinds of activities. Cockers love people and enjoy showing off, so they excel in dog shows, as well as in obedience and agility. True to their original purpose, they are excellent gun dogs. A strong attachment to their people means that they will want to share your space all the time. They also owe at least some of their good looks to their abundant hair, which will require regular grooming and will, no matter how much you try to control it, end up on your furniture.

COMPETITION

From the exquisite conformation exhibition dog to a hard-working go-all-day gun dog, Cockers are a can-do breed, eligible to compete in all companion events, as well as in spaniel field trials and hunting tests. With their soft hair, gentle nature, and sweet expressions, they are exquisite therapy dogs.

Official Standard for the Cocker Spaniel

General Appearance: The Cocker Spaniel is the smallest member of the Sporting Group. He has a sturdy, compact body and a cleanly chiseled and refined head, with the overall dog in complete balance and of ideal size. He stands well up at the shoulder on straight forelegs with a topline sloping slightly toward strong, moderately bent, muscular quarters. He is a dog capable of considerable speed, combined with great endurance. Above all, he must be free and merry, sound, well balanced throughout and in action show a keen inclination to work. A dog well balanced in all parts is more desirable than a dog with strongly contrasting good points and faults.

Size, Proportion, Substance: *Size*—The ideal height at the withers for an adult dog is 15 inches and for an adult bitch, 14 inches. Height may vary one-half inch above or below this ideal. A dog whose height exceeds 15½ inches or a bitch whose height exceeds 14½ inches shall be disqualified. An adult dog whose height is less than 14½ inches and an adult bitch whose height is less than 13½ inches shall be penalized. Height is determined by a line perpendicular to the ground from the top of the shoulder blades, the dog standing naturally with its forelegs and lower hind legs parallel to the line of measurement. *Proportion*—The measurement from the breast bone to back of thigh is slightly longer than the measurement from the highest point of withers to the ground. The body must be of sufficient length to permit a straight and free stride; the dog never appears long and low.

Head: To attain a well-proportioned *head*, which must be in balance with the rest of the dog, it

AKC Official Guide to Sporting Dogs

embodies the following: *Expression*—The expression is intelligent, alert, soft and appealing. *Eyes*—Eyeballs are round and full and look directly forward. The shape of the eye rims gives a slightly almond shaped appearance; the eye is not weak or goggled. The color of the iris is dark brown and in general the darker the better. Disqualifications: Eye(s) blue, blue marbled, blue flecked. *Ears*—Lobular, long, of fine leather, well feathered, and placed no higher than a line to the lower part of the eye. *Skull*—Rounded but not exaggerated with no tendency toward flatness; the eyebrows are clearly defined with a pronounced stop. The bony structure beneath the eyes is well chiseled with no prominence in the cheeks. The muzzle is broad and deep, with square even jaws. To be in correct balance, the distance from the stop to the tip of the nose is one half the distance from the stop up over the crown to the base of the skull. Nose—of sufficient size to balance the *muzzle* and foreface, with well developed nostrils typical of a sporting dog. It is black in color in the blacks, black and tans, and black and whites; in other colors it may be brown, liver or black, the darker the better. The color of nose harmonizes with the color of the eye rim. Lips—The upper lip is full and of sufficient depth to cover the lower jaw. Teeth—Teeth strong and sound, not too small and meet in a scissors *bite*.

Neck, Topline, Body: *Neck*—The neck is sufficiently long to allow the nose to reach the ground easily, muscular and free from pendulous "throatiness." It rises strongly from the shoulders and arches slightly as it tapers to join the head. *Topline*—sloping slightly toward muscular quarters. *Body*—The chest is deep, its lowest point no higher than the elbows, its front sufficiently wide for adequate heart and lung space, yet not so wide as to interfere with the straightforward movement of the forelegs. Ribs are deep and well sprung. Back is strong and sloping evenly and slightly downward from the shoulders to the set-on of the docked tail. The docked *tail* is set on and carried on a line with the topline of the back, or slightly higher; never straight up like a Terrier and never so low as to indicate timidity. When the dog is in motion the tail action is merry.

Forequarters: The shoulders are well laid back forming an angle with the upper arm of approximately 90 degrees which permits the dog to move his forelegs in an easy manner with forward reach. Shoulders are clean-cut and sloping without protrusion and so set that the upper points of the withers are at an angle which permits a wide spring of rib. When viewed from the side with the forelegs vertical, the elbow is directly below the highest point of the shoulder blade. Forelegs are parallel, straight, strongly boned and muscular and set close to the body well under the scapulae. The pasterns are short and strong. Dewclaws on forelegs may be removed. Feet compact, large, round and firm with horny pads; they turn neither in nor out.

Hindquarters: Hips are wide and quarters well rounded and muscular. When viewed from behind, the hind legs are parallel when in motion and at rest. The hind legs are strongly boned, and muscled with moderate angulation at the stifle and powerful, clearly defined thighs. The stifle is strong and there is no slippage of it in motion or when standing. The hocks are strong and well let down. Dewclaws on hind legs may be removed.

Coat: On the head, short and fine; on the body, medium length, with enough undercoating to give protection. The ears, chest, abdomen and legs are well feathered, but not so excessively as to hide the Cocker Spaniel's true lines and movement or affect his appearance and function as a moderately coated sporting dog. The texture is most important. The coat is silky, flat or slightly wavy and of a texture which permits easy care. Excessive coat or curly or cottony textured coat shall be severely penalized. Use of electric clippers on the back coat is not desirable. Trimming to enhance the dog's true lines should be done to appear as natural as possible.

Color and Markings: *Black Variety*—Solid color black to include black with tan points. The black should be jet; shadings of brown or liver in the coat are not desirable. A small amount of white on the chest and/or throat is allowed; white in any other location shall disqualify.

Any Solid Color Other than Black (ASCOB)— Any solid color other than black, ranging from lightest cream to darkest red, including brown and brown with tan points. The color shall be of a uniform shade, but lighter color of the feathering is permissible. A small amount of white on the chest and/or throat is allowed; white in any other location shall disqualify.

Parti-Color Variety—Two or more solid, well broken colors, one of which must be white; black and white, red and white (the red may range from lightest cream to darkest red), brown and white, and roans, to include any such color combination with tan points. It is preferable that the tan markings be located in the same pattern as for the tan points in the Black and ASCOB varieties. Roans are classified as parti-colors and may be of any of the usual roaning patterns. Primary color which is ninety percent (90%) or more shall disqualify. *Tan Points*—The color of the tan may be from the lightest cream to the darkest red and is restricted to ten percent (10%) or less of the color of the specimen; tan markings in excess of that amount shall disqualify. In the case of tan points in the Black or ASCOB variety, the markings shall be located as follows:

    1) A clear tan spot over each eye;
    2) On the sides of the muzzle and on the cheeks;
    3) On the underside of the ears;
    4) On all feet and/or legs;
    5) Under the tail;
    6) On the chest, optional; presence or absence shall not be penalized.

Tan markings which are not readily visible or which amount only to traces, shall be penalized. Tan on the muzzle which extends upward, over and joins shall also be penalized. The absence of tan markings in the Black or ASCOB variety in any of the specified locations in any otherwise tan-pointed dog shall disqualify.

Gait: The Cocker Spaniel, though the smallest of the sporting dogs, possesses a typical sporting dog gait. Prerequisite to good movement is balance between the front and rear assemblies. He drives with strong, powerful rear quarters and is properly constructed in the shoulders and forelegs so that he can reach forward without constriction in a full stride to counterbalance the driving force from the rear. Above all, his gait is coordinated, smooth and effortless. The dog must cover ground with his action; excessive animation should not be mistaken for proper gait.

Temperament: Equable in temperament with no suggestion of timidity.

Disqualifications: *Height—Males over 15½ inches; females over 14½ inches. Eye(s) blue, blue marbled, blue flecked. Color and Markings—The aforementioned colors are the only acceptable colors or combination of colors. Any other colors or combination of colors to disqualify. Black Variety—White markings except on chest and throat. Any Solid Color Other than Black Variety—White markings except on chest and throat. Parti-color Variety—Primary color ninety percent (90%) or more. Tan Points—(1) Tan markings in excess of ten percent (10%); (2) Absence of tan markings in Black or ASCOB Variety in any of the specified locations in an otherwise tan-pointed dog.*

Approved January 9, 2018
Effective March 1, 2018

Cocker Spaniel

AKC Official Guide to Sporting Dogs

Meet the Curly-Coated Retriever

Recognized by AKC® in 1924
Curly-Coated Retriever Club of America (ccrca.org), formed in 1979

Traits
- Energetic
- Proud
- Wickedly Smart

HISTORY

Developed in England as both a waterfowl retriever and upland game hunter, the Curly-Coated Retriever is known for his innate field ability, courage, and perseverance. Distinguished by his coat of small, tight, water-resistant, crisp curls, the Curly-Coated Retriever is strong, robust, and agile, willing to work as long as there is work to be done, retrieving game in the heaviest of cover and iciest of waters.

In the absence of early records, the origin of the Curly-Coated Retriever remains a matter of conjecture, but there appears little doubt that it is one of the oldest breeds now classified as retrievers. There is good evidence that the breed existed in the English countryside as early as 1490, possibly earlier. Believed to be descended from an old type of close-curled English water dog, writers of the period praised the exceptional retrieving powers and intelligence of these dogs along with their fondness of water and sagacity.

Several breeds that may have played a role in the early evolution of the Curly-Coated Retriever include the Greenland Dog and St. John's Newfoundland. Now extinct, the Tweed Water Spaniel and Llanidloes Welsh Setter, both with densely curled, waterproof coats, were probably used to enhance the breed. Given considerable trade with continental Europe and within the British Isles over several centuries, crossbreeding with other developing hunting breeds was inevitable. Throughout the varied breed crosses, the dominant genetic characteristics such as the smooth hair of the face, the tightly curled body coat, and the sturdy frame were maintained.

By the early 1800s, the Curly-Coated Retriever had achieved the consistent type that we see today. The Curly was first exhibited at dog shows in Birmingham, England, in 1860. The first breed club for the Curly-Coated Retriever was formed in England in 1896.

Documentation supports that the breed was in the United States as early as the mid-1800s and possibly earlier, although the first Curly-Coated Retriever was not registered with the AKC® Stud Book until 1924. Throughout the early 1900s, the Curly remained a popular gun dog because his ability to adapt to various hunting situations was almost legendary. Although the breed fell out of favor during World War II, the Curly experienced a resurgence of interest in the United States beginning in 1966 and has developed a small but passionate following.

FORM AND FUNCTION

These versatile hunters are sturdy, agile, muscular, and moderately built. Their unique water-resistant coat is smooth, short, and straight on the face and forehead; thick, crisp, and curly on the body; with looser curls on the ears.

LIVING WITH A CURLY

An energetic and intelligent dog, the Curly is an excellent companion for a family with an active lifestyle, but he requires training and daily exercise. This is a breed that enjoys human interaction and hence is never happy being relegated to a backyard with only occasional human contact. The Curly wants to be part of the family. As one of the more independent retrieving breeds, the Curly may appear somewhat aloof with strangers, but he is always willing to please and is affectionate with his family.

This breed is the tallest (23 to 27 inches at the withers) of the retrievers and hence will be a large dog (65 to 100 pounds, depending on the sex). Early socialization and training are necessary to ensure a happy, well-adjusted Curly. As a slow-maturing breed, puppyhood can last well past twelve months, and a dog may not fully mature until at least three years of age. Patience and a sense of humor are needed to raise a Curly puppy to adulthood.

As a single-coated breed with no undercoat or fur—only hair—the coat is very easy to care for, requiring only occasional bathing and slight trimming. The breed does shed hair, and the amount of shedding varies with the seasons and local climatic conditions.

Known for his hunting ability, the Curly makes a good choice for the avid recreational hunter who also maintains a family home environment. Early exposure to birds and retrieving will allow the Curly puppy to expend unwanted energy and stimulate the puppy's innate hunting and retrieving desires.

COMPETITION

Curly-Coated Retrievers participate in retriever hunting tests and field trials, spaniel hunting tests, agility, tracking, obedience, rally, and conformation events.

Official Standard for the Curly-Coated Retriever

General Appearance: This smartly upstanding, multipurpose hunting retriever is recognized by most canine historians as one of the oldest of the retrieving breeds. Developed in England, the Curly was long a favorite of English gamekeepers. Prized for innate field ability, courage and indomitable perseverance, a correctly built and tempered Curly will work as long as there is work to be done, retrieving both fur and feather in the heaviest of cover and the iciest of waters. To work all day a Curly must be balanced and sound, strong and robust, and quick and agile. Outline, carriage and attitude all combine for a grace and elegance somewhat uncommon among the other retriever breeds, providing the unique, upstanding quality desired in the breed. In outline, the Curly is moderately angulated front and rear and, when comparing height to length, gives the impression of being higher on leg than the other retriever breeds. In carriage, the Curly is an erect, alert, self-confident dog. In motion, all parts blend into a smooth, powerful, harmonious symmetry. The coat, a hallmark of the breed, is of great importance for all Curlies, whether companion, hunting or show dogs. The perfect coat is a dense mass of small, tight, distinct, crisp curls. The Curly is wickedly smart and highly trainable and, as such, is cherished as much for his role as loyal companion at home as he is in the field.

Size, Proportion, Substance: Ideal height at withers: dogs, 25 to 27 inches; bitches, 23 to 25 inches. A

Curly-Coated Retriever

clearly superior Curly falling outside of this range should not be penalized because of size. The body proportions are slightly off square, meaning that the dog is slightly longer from prosternum to buttocks as he is from withers to ground. The Curly is both sturdy and elegant. The degree of substance is sufficient to ensure strength and endurance without sacrificing grace. Bone and substance are neither spindly nor massive and should be in proportion with weight and height and balanced throughout.

Head: The head is a longer-than-wide wedge, readily distinguishable from that of all other retriever breeds, and of a size in balance with the body. Length of foreface is equal, or nearly equal, to length of backskull and, when viewed in profile, the planes are parallel. The stop is shallow and sloping. At the point of joining, the width of foreface may be slightly less than the width of the backskull but blending of the two should be smooth. The head has a nearly straight, continuous taper to the nose and is clean cut, not coarse, blocky or cheeky. *Expression*—Intelligent and alert. *Eyes*—Almond-shaped, rather large but not too prominent. Black or brown in black dogs and brown or amber in liver dogs. Harsh yellow eyes and loose haws are undesirable. *Ears*—Rather small, set on a line slightly above the corner of the eye, and lying close to the head. *Backskull*—Flat or nearly flat. *Foreface*—*Muzzle* is wedge-shaped with no hint of snipiness. The taper ends mildly, neither acutely pointed nor bluntly squared-off but rather slightly rounding at the bottom. Mouth is level and never wry. Jaws are long and strong. A scissors bite is preferred. Teeth set straight and even. The lips are tight and clean, not pendulous. The nose is fully pigmented; black on black dogs, brown on liver dogs. Nostrils are large.

Neck, Topline, Body: *Neck*—Strong and slightly arched, of medium length, free from throatiness and flowing freely into moderately laid-back shoulders. *Backline*—The back, that portion of the body from the rear point of the withers to the beginning of the loin, is strong and level. The loin, that part of the body extending from the end of the rib cage to the start of the pelvis, is short and muscular. The croup, that portion of the body from the start of the pelvis to the tail set-on, is only slightly sloping. *Body*—Chest is decidedly deep and not too wide, oval in cross-section, with brisket reaching elbow. While the impression of the chest should be of depth not width, the chest is not pinched or narrow. The ribs are well-sprung, neither barrel-shaped nor slab-sided, and extend well back into a deep, powerful loin with a moderate tuck-up of flank. *Tail*—Carried straight or fairly straight, never docked, and reaching approximately to the hock. Never curled over the back and should not be kinked or crooked. Covered with curls and, if trimmed, tapering toward the point.

Forequarters: Shoulder blades are very long, well covered with muscle, and are moderately laid back at about a 55 degree angle. The width between shoulder blades is adequate to allow enough flexibility to easily retrieve game. Upper arm bones are about equal in length with shoulder blades and laid back at approximately the same angle as the blades, meaning the forelegs are set under the withers. The equal length of shoulder blade and upper arm bone and the balanced angulation between the two allows for good extension of the front legs. The forelegs are straight with strong, true pasterns. Feet are round and compact, with well-arched toes and thick pads. Front dewclaws are generally removed.

Hindquarters: Strong and in balance with front angulation. Thighs are powerful with muscling carrying well down into the second thigh. Stifle is of moderate bend. The hocks are strong and true, turning neither in nor out, with hock joint well let down. Rear dewclaws are generally removed.

Coat: The coat is a distinguishing characteristic and quite different from that of any other breed. The body coat is a thick mass of small, tight, crisp curls, lying close to the skin, resilient, water resistant, and of sufficient density to provide protection against weather, water and punishing cover. Curls also extend up the entire neck to the occiput, down the thigh and back leg to at least the hock, and over the entire tail. Elsewhere, the coat is short, smooth and straight, including on the forehead, face, front of forelegs, and feet. A patch of uncurled hair behind the withers or bald patches anywhere on the body, including bald strips down the back of the legs or a triangular bald patch on the throat, should be severely penalized. A looser, more open curl is acceptable on the ears. Sparse, silky, fuzzy or very harsh, dry or brittle hair is a fault. *Trimming*— Feathering may be trimmed from the ears, belly, backs of forelegs, thighs, pasterns, hocks, and feet. On the tail, feathering should be removed. Short trimming of the coat on the ear is permitted but shearing of the body coat is undesirable.

Color: Black or liver. Either color is correct. A prominent white patch is undesirable but a few white hairs are allowable in an otherwise good dog.

Gait: The dual function of the Curly as both waterfowl retriever and upland game hunter demands a dog who moves with strength and power yet is quick and agile. The ground-covering stride is a well-coordinated melding of grace and power, neither mincing nor lumbering. The seemingly effortless trot is efficient and balanced front to rear. When viewed from the side, the reach in front and rear is free-flowing, not stilted or hackneyed. When viewed from the front or rear, movement is true: the front legs turn neither in nor out and the rear legs do not cross. Well-developed, muscular thighs and strong hocks do their full share of work, contributing to rear thrust and drive. The extension in front is strong and smooth and in balance with rear action. Balance in structure translates to balance in movement and is of great importance to ensure soundness and endurance; extremes of angulation and gait are not desirable.

Temperament: Self-confident, steadfast and proud, this active, intelligent dog is a charming and gentle family companion and a determined, durable hunter. The Curly is alert, biddable and responsive to family and friends, whether at home or in the field. Of independent nature and discerning intelligence, a Curly sometimes appears aloof or self-willed, and, as such, is often less demonstrative, particularly toward strangers, than the other retriever breeds. The Curly's independence and poise should not be confused with shyness or a lack of willingness to please. In the show ring, a correctly tempered Curly will steadily stand his ground, submit easily to examination, and might or might not wag his tail when doing so. In the field, the Curly is eager, persistent and inherently courageous. At home, he is calm and affectionate. Shyness is a fault and any dog who shies away from show ring examination should be penalized. Minor allowances can be made for puppies who misbehave in the show ring due to overexuberance or lack of training or experience.

Approved October 12, 1993
Effective November 30, 1993

Curly-Coated Retriever

AKC Official Guide to Sporting Dogs

Meet the English Cocker Spaniel

Recognized by AKC® in 1946
English Cocker Spaniel Club of America (englishcocker.org), formed in 1936

Traits
- Energetic
- Versatile
- Responsive

HISTORY

Until the twentieth century, *spaniel* was a generic term for dogs who were used to hunt and flush a variety of game birds. The smaller dogs were called cockers and were used to hunt woodcock. Larger dogs, often from the same litter, were called springers because they flushed or "sprang" birds from cover. In Britain, as fanciers bred for either the smaller or larger dogs, several separate breeds were developed. In the United States, the Cocker Spaniel breed developed somewhat differently from its British cousin. By the 1930s, two distinct breeds were emerging. In 1946, with approval from both parent clubs, the AKC® divided them into two distinct breeds, the Cocker Spaniel and the English Cocker Spaniel, which remained true to its origins. Outside the United States, the English Cocker Spaniel is known as the Cocker Spaniel, while our Cocker Spaniel is known as the American Cocker Spaniel.

FORM AND FUNCTION

The English Cocker Spaniel is a compactly built, active, merry sporting dog who is often considered to be a "large dog in a small package." English Cocker Spaniels come in a wide variety of coat colors, both solid and parti-color. Bred to flush and retrieve upland game birds, they possess the structure to allow them to easily penetrate dense cover and upland terrain. Well balanced, without exaggeration, they cover ground effortlessly and energetically. English Cocker Spaniels are versatile hunters, engaging family companions, impressive show dogs, and noteworthy performance competitors.

LIVING WITH AN ENGLISH COCKER

Potential owners visiting a breeder should be willing to sit on the floor and play with the litter. The litter should be clean, well groomed, robust, and healthy in appearance. In addition, they should be curious and eager to meet new friends. Give serious consideration to the puppy who is interested in you! A well-socialized puppy will relax and seem at home when you hold him in your lap. Meet the sire and dam of the litter if possible. Ask questions of the breeder; a good breeder will take the time to answer them all, now and after you take the puppy home. English Cocker Spaniels are "people" dogs and enjoy activities with their owners. Happiness is having a job to do, whether it's a day's hunt in the woods or snuggling next to you on the sofa. If you yearn for a dog who wants to share all aspects of your life, the English Cocker Spaniel is ready to oblige. The breed's versatility, intelligence, athleticism, and willingness to work make the English Cocker Spaniel an ideal choice for owners who enjoy a high degree of interaction and attention from their canine companion. Socialization of puppies and young adults is highly recommended. The English Cocker is normally highly food motivated and often bored with repetitive training or sequencing. Variety and creativity are mandatory when training the English Cocker Spaniel. Performance is enhanced when training is reinforced in a positive and enthusiastic manner. The breed requires regular grooming and frequent brushing of its moderate coat. Special attention must be paid to the dog's long ears, keeping them clean and neatly trimmed. Daily exercise is good for dog and owner if possible, and mandatory if conditioning for the show, field, or performance work.

English Cockers are generally very healthy and long-lived dogs. The breed ages well, maintaining an active lifestyle well into their senior years.

COMPETITION

English Cockers participate in many AKC® events—conformation shows, spaniel field trials and hunting tests, obedience, rally, and agility trials. Possessing a keen nose, English Cockers are excellent trackers. Many English Cockers thrive on the variety of events available and earn titles in multiple venues.

Official Standard for the English Cocker Spaniel

General Appearance: The English Cocker Spaniel is an active, merry sporting dog, standing well up at the withers and compactly built. He is alive with energy; his gait is powerful and frictionless, capable both of covering ground effortlessly and penetrating dense cover to flush and retrieve game. His enthusiasm in the field and the incessant action of his tail while at work indicate how much he enjoys the hunting for which he was bred. His head is especially characteristic. He is, above all, a dog of balance, both standing and moving, without exaggeration in any part, the whole worth more than the sum of its parts.

Size, Proportion, Substance: *Size*—Height at withers: males 16 to 17 inches; females 15 to 16 inches. Deviations to be penalized. The most desirable weights: males, 28 to 34 pounds; females, 26 to 32 pounds. Proper conformation and substance should be considered more important than weight alone. *Proportion*—Compactly built and short-coupled, with height at withers slightly greater than the distance from withers to set-on of tail. *Substance*—The English Cocker is a solidly built dog with as much bone and substance as is possible without becoming cloddy or coarse.

Head: General appearance: strong, yet free from coarseness, softly contoured, without sharp angles. Taken as a whole, the parts combine to produce the expression distinctive of the breed. *Expression*—Soft, melting, yet dignified, alert, and intelligent. *Eyes*—The eyes are essential to the desired expression. They are medium in size,

full and slightly oval; set wide apart; lids tight. Haws are inconspicuous; may be pigmented or unpigmented. Eye color dark brown, except in livers and liver parti-colors where hazel is permitted, but the darker the hazel the better. *Ears*—Set low, lying close to the head; leather fine, extending to the nose, well covered with long, silky, straight or slightly wavy hair. *Skull*—Arched and slightly flattened when seen both from the side and from the front. Viewed in profile, the brow appears not appreciably higher than the backskull. Viewed from above, the sides of the skull are in planes roughly parallel to those of the muzzle. Stop definite, but moderate, and slightly grooved. *Muzzle*—Equal in length to skull; well cushioned; only as much narrower than the skull as is consistent with a full eye placement; cleanly chiseled under the eyes. Jaws strong, capable of carrying game. Nostrils wide for proper development of scenting ability; color black, except in livers and parti-colors of that shade where they will be brown; reds and parti-colors of that shade may be brown, but black is preferred. Lips square, but not pendulous or showing prominent flews. *Bite*—Scissors. A level bite is not preferred. Overshot or undershot to be severely penalized.

Neck, Topline, and Body: *Neck*—Graceful and muscular, arched toward the head and blending cleanly, without throatiness, into sloping shoulders; moderate in length and in balance with the length and height of the dog. *Topline*—The line of the neck blends into the shoulder and backline in a smooth curve. The backline slopes very slightly toward a gently rounded croup, and is free from sagging or rumpiness. *Body*—Compact and well-knit, giving the impression of strength without heaviness. Chest deep; not so wide as to interfere with action of forelegs, nor so narrow as to allow the front to appear narrow or pinched. Forechest well developed, prosternum projecting moderately beyond shoulder points. Brisket reaches to the elbow and slopes gradually to a moderate tuck-up. Ribs well sprung and springing gradually to mid-body, tapering to back ribs which are of good depth and extend well back. Back short and strong. Loin short, broad and very slightly arched, but not enough to affect the topline appreciably. Croup gently rounded, without any tendency to fall away sharply. *Tail*—Docked. Set on to conform to croup. Ideally, the tail is carried horizontally and is in constant motion while the dog is in action. Under excitement, the dog may carry his tail somewhat higher, but not cocked up.

Forequarters: The English Cocker is moderately angulated. Shoulders are sloping, the blade flat and smoothly fitting. Shoulder blade and upper arm are approximately equal in length. Upper arm set well back, joining the shoulder with sufficient angulation to place the elbow beneath the highest point of the shoulder blade when the dog is standing naturally. *Forelegs*—Straight, with bone nearly uniform in size from elbow to heel; elbows set close to the body; pasterns nearly straight, with some flexibility. *Feet*—Proportionate in size to the legs, firm, round and catlike; toes arched and tight; pads thick.

Hindquarters: Angulation moderate and, most importantly, in balance with that of the forequarters. Hips relatively broad and well rounded. Upper thighs broad, thick and muscular, providing plenty of propelling power. Second thighs well muscled and approximately equal in length to the upper. Stifle strong and well bent. Hock to pad short. Feet as in front.

Coat: On head, short and fine; of medium length on body; flat or slightly wavy; silky in texture. The English Cocker is well-feathered, but not so profusely as to interfere with field work. Trimming is permitted to remove overabundant hair and to enhance the dog's true lines. It should be done so as to appear as natural as possible.

Color: Various. Parti-colors are either clearly marked, ticked or roaned, the white appearing in combination with black, liver or shades of red. In parti-colors it is preferable that solid markings be broken on the body and more or less evenly distributed; absence of body markings is acceptable. Solid colors are black, liver or shades of red. White feet on a solid are undesirable; a little white on throat is acceptable; but in neither case do these white markings make the dog a parti-color. Tan markings, clearly defined and of rich shade, may appear in conjunction with black, livers and parti-color combinations of those colors. Black and tans and liver and tans are considered solid colors.

Gait: The English Cocker is capable of hunting in dense cover and upland terrain. His gait is accordingly characterized more by drive and the appearance of power than by great speed. He covers ground effortlessly and with extension both in front and in rear, appropriate to his angulation. In the ring, he carries his head proudly and is able to keep much the same topline while in action as when standing for examination. Going and coming, he moves in a straight line without crabbing or rolling, and with width between both front and rear legs appropriate to his build and gait.

Temperament: The English Cocker is merry and affectionate, of equable disposition, neither sluggish nor hyperactive, a willing worker and a faithful and engaging companion.

Approved October 11, 1988
Effective November 30, 1988

English Cocker Spaniel

AKC Official Guide to Sporting Dogs

Meet the English Setter

Recognized by AKC® in 1878
English Setter Association of America (esaa.com), formed in 1931

Traits
- Playful
- Friendly
- Gentle

HISTORY

The exact origin of the elegant and gentle English Setter isn't known, but dogs of this kind, which crouched and "set" to indicate birds, are described by Dr. John Caius, physician to Queen Elizabeth I, in his 1570 book *Of Englishe Dogges*. "Another sort of Dogges be there, serviceable for fowling. … When he aprocheth near to the place where the bird is, he lays him down, and with a mark of his paws betrayeth the place of the birds last abode, whereby it is supposed that this kind of dogge is called Setter." Caius then goes on to describe how the fowler would open and toss a net over the dog and the birds to catch them. Setters were also frequently used to hunt with falcons at this time. With the advent of hunting with firearms, the English Setter was adapted to hunting with a more upright stance instead of crouching.

In the nineteenth century, British sportsman and breeder Edward Laverack did much to create the modern English Setter we know today. He maintained his own line of dogs for some thirty-five years, and many of his dogs formed the basis of our show lines today in the United States. Fellow breeder Purcell Llewellin, starting with dogs from Laverack, bred many outstanding English Setters for the field. Many of Llewellin's dogs were also imported to America. The English Setter was one of the original nine breeds recognized by the American Kennel Club® in 1884. The first dog registered by the AKC® was an English Setter named Adonis. Today the breed is a beloved companion dog, still capable of doing his job in the field. English Setters are known for their beauty, but they are always keen when it comes to birds. Perhaps the only thing they love more than birds is their family.

FORM AND FUNCTION

The graceful English Setter was developed to find birds in the field, working closely with the hunter. The breed's white coat with belton markings makes the dogs easy to see in the field. The parallel planes of the head are designed to help the dogs take in scent through their air passages. The breed's fairly pendant flews and moderately long ears help pick up scent. The dog's medium size and efficient, ground-covering stride allow him to hunt at a good pace for the hunter. The English Setter does not hunt as far afield or as close as some other breeds. Silky feathering protects them from brush and briars in the field. The breed's mild, pleasing temperament enables it to form a close bond with owners, which is desirable for a bird dog.

LIVING WITH AN ENGLISH SETTER

Puppies are born white and develop their spots, or belton flecking, as they get older. All colors are equally good: blue belton, orange belton, tricolor, liver belton, and lemon belton. These last two colors are rather rare, but they do occur. Some puppies are roan (coloring all over), and some have patches. Talk to the breeder and be honest about whether you are looking for a pet or a show puppy. English Setter puppies usually go home with their new owners when they are eight to twelve weeks old. The ideal English Setter owner will have plenty of time for the puppy as he grows up and will spend time with the dog as an adult. English Setters love to be with people, and they do not do well if they are ignored. They need to have time indoors with the family and are great with children. English Setters are playful and fun-loving

throughout their lives, even when they get older. Ideally, an owner will also have a fenced yard, as English Setters need lots of daily exercise and room to run. With their medium-long coats, they also need to be brushed and combed two or three times per week to avoid matting. English Setters are not hard to train and respond best to positive reinforcement—never harsh methods.

COMPETITION

The English Setter possesses the ideal blend of strength, stamina, grace, and style, and he excels at conformation dog shows, obedience, rally, and agility trials. English Setters can also participate in tracking and lure coursing, as well as in pointing dog hunting tests and field trials, at which they are naturals. Many make excellent personal hunting dogs as well as wonderful therapy dogs. English Setters love doing things with their owners, so find something you and your dog enjoy doing and have fun with it.

Official Standard for the English Setter

General Appearance: An elegant, substantial and symmetrical gun dog suggesting the ideal blend of strength, stamina, grace, and style. Flat-coated with feathering of good length. Gaiting freely and smoothly with long forward reach, strong rear drive and firm topline. Males decidedly masculine without coarseness. Females decidedly feminine without over-refinement. Overall appearance, balance, gait, and purpose to be given more emphasis than any component part. Above all, extremes of anything distort type and must be faulted.

Head: Size and proportion in harmony with body. Long and lean with a well defined stop. When viewed from the side, head planes (top of muzzle, top of skull and bottom of lower jaw) are parallel. *Skull*—Oval when viewed from above, of medium width, without coarseness, and only slightly wider at the earset than at the brow. Moderately defined occipital protuberance. Length of skull from occiput to stop equal in length of muzzle. *Muzzle*—Long and square when viewed from the side, of good depth with flews squared and fairly pendant. Width in harmony with width of skull and equal at nose and stop. Level from eyes to tip of nose. *Nose*—Black or dark brown, fully pigmented. Nostrils wide apart and large. ***Foreface***—Skeletal structure under the eyes well chiseled with no suggestion of fullness. Cheeks present a smooth and clean-cut appearance. ***Teeth***—Close scissors bite preferred. Even bite acceptable. ***Eyes***—Dark brown, the darker the better. Bright, and spaced to give a mild and intelligent expression. Nearly round, fairly large, neither deepset nor protruding. Eyelid rims dark and fully pigmented. Lids fit tightly so that haw is not exposed. ***Ears***—Set well back and low, even with or below eye level. When relaxed carried close to the head. Of moderate length, slightly rounded at the ends, moderately thin leather, and covered with silky hair.

Neck and Body: ***Neck***—Long and graceful, muscular and lean. Arched at the crest and cleancut where it joins the head at the base of the skull. Larger and more muscular toward the shoulders, with the base of the neck flowing smoothly into the shoulders. Not too throaty. ***Topline***—In motion or standing appears level or sloping slightly downward without sway or drop from withers to tail forming a graceful outline of medium length. ***Forechest***—Well developed, point of sternum projecting slightly in front of point of shoulder/upper arm joint. ***Chest***—Deep, but not so wide or round as to interfere with the action of the forelegs. Brisket deep enough to reach the level of the elbow. ***Ribs***—Long, springing gradually to the middle of the body, then tapering as they approach the end of the chest cavity. ***Back***—Straight and strong at its junction with loin. ***Loin***—Strong, moderate in length, slightly arched. Tuck up moderate. ***Hips***—Croup nearly flat. Hip bones wide apart, hips rounded and blending smoothly into hind legs. ***Tail***—A smooth continuation of the topline. Tapering to a fine point with only sufficient length to reach the hock joint or slightly less. Carried straight and level with the back. Feathering straight and silky, hanging loosely in a fringe.

Forequarters: ***Shoulder***—Shoulder blade well laid back. Upper arm equal in length to and forming a nearly right angle with the shoulder blade. Shoulders fairly close together at the tips. Shoulder blades lie flat and meld smoothly with contours of body. ***Forelegs***—From front or side, forelegs straight and parallel. Elbows have no tendency

to turn in or out when standing or gaiting. Arm flat and muscular. Bone substantial but not coarse and muscles hard and devoid of flabbiness. *Pasterns*—Short, strong and nearly round with the slope deviating very slightly forward from the perpendicular. *Feet*—Face directly forward. Toes closely set, strong and well arched. Pads well developed and tough. Dewclaws may be removed.

Hindquarters: Wide, muscular thighs and well developed lower thighs. Pelvis equal in length to and forming a nearly right angle with upper thigh. In balance with forequarter assembly. Stifle well bent and strong. Lower thigh only slightly longer than upper thigh. Hock joint well bent and strong. Rear pastern short, strong, nearly round and perpendicular to the ground. Hind legs, when seen from the rear, straight and parallel to each other. Hock joints have no tendency to turn in or out when standing or gaiting.

Coat: Flat without curl or wooliness. Feathering on ears, chest, abdomen, underside of thighs, back of all legs and on the tail of good length but not so excessive as to hide true lines and movement or to affect the dog's appearance or function as a sporting dog.

Markings and Color: *Markings*—White ground color with intermingling of darker hairs resulting in belton markings varying in degree from clear distinct flecking to roan shading, but flecked all over preferred. Head and ear patches acceptable, heavy patches of color on the body undesirable. *Color*—Orange belton, blue belton (white with black markings), tricolor (blue belton with tan on muzzle, over the eyes and on the legs), lemon belton, liver belton.

Movement and Carriage: An effortless graceful movement demonstrating endurance while covering ground efficiently. Long forward reach and strong rear drive with a lively tail and a proud head carriage. Head may be carried slightly lower when moving to allow for greater reach of forelegs. The back strong, firm, and free of roll. When moving at a trot, as speed increases, the legs tend to converge toward a line representing the center of gravity.

Size: Dogs about 25 inches; bitches about 24 inches.

Temperament: Gentle, affectionate, friendly, without shyness, fear or viciousness.

Approved November 11, 1986

Meet the English Springer Spaniel

Recognized by AKC® in 1910
English Springer Spaniel Field Trial Association (essfta.org), formed in 1927

Traits
- Patient
- Loving
- Playful

HISTORY

Breed scholars speculate that dogs of spaniel type originated in Spain, hence the name. Research by long-time English Springer enthusiast, scholar, and educator Francie Nelson indicates that it is more likely that spaniels, along with other dog types, originated in Asia and migrated west, across northern Europe and beyond. The Old German noun, *span*, has several meanings, among them "a brace of two animals working together." Artwork and writings from Europe, notably the Netherlands and France, depict dogs of spaniel type. Although their true origin is unknown, spaniels go back at least to the fourteenth century, but are no doubt much older.

English Springers were refined in England, as the breed's name suggests. Travel—whether over land or water—was difficult and time-consuming. Varieties within breeds developed regionally. The land spaniel on one English estate could look quite different from the land spaniel on another English estate. Spaniels on the estate of the Duke of Norfolk were called "Norfolk Spaniels"; spaniels from Sussex were "Sussex Spaniels"; and spaniels from Clumber Park were Clumber Spaniels. "Springer" and "Cocker" described hunting function or game hunted. The term *field spaniel* was generic and described them all.

The first known standard for English Springer Spaniels was drafted in the breed's country of origin, England; the breed was recognized there in 1902. The first US breed standard was drafted in 1927 and revised in 1932, and then again in the 1950s, 1970s, and 1990s.

FORM AND FUNCTION

The English Springer Spaniel developed as a mid-sized, compact, sturdy hunter with outstanding ability to find, flush, and fetch game in heavy cover. The English Springer's kind, trusting, and tractable nature brought him from the field into the home, where he happily remains. The UK and US standards describe well the English Springer's essential characteristics: sturdy bone and rib spring, pendulous ears, liver and white or black and white markings (with or without ticking, and with or without tan points), unique alert yet kind expression and temperament, easy movement, and the heart and endurance to do a day's work in the field or to keep up with an active human family.

LIVING WITH AN ENGLISH SPRINGER

Purchase your English Springer Spaniel from a private, small-scale hobby breeder with years of expertise, a love for the breed, and a commitment to its healthy future. Study the breed, meet its people at competitive events, discuss health concerns, and then establish a relationship with a breeder. This relationship should support you throughout the life of your English Springer.

Flexible, patient, and loving, ideal owners are committed to the breed's long life span (twelve-plus years) and engaged in building a lifetime of enjoyable activities with their dogs. Puppies need socialization and training to become great dog citizens, and ideal owners will provide that—along with health care, grooming, and the personal attention that these dogs crave. An English Springer, with proper exercise, can live in a small home or apartment, but a large fenced yard is ideal. English Springers are groomed to remove dead undercoat, to prevent mats, and to keep the coat healthy and shining. Pendulous ears are easily infected and must be kept clean. Puppy training is important, ensuring that your English Springer assumes an appropriate role as a member of your household. English Springers are quick and highly intelligent; continued training and gentle guidance are important. Be sure that you, the leader of your English Springer's pack, are in control at all times, because the English Springer is an active and forward explorer of his environment.

COMPETITION

The English Springer Spaniel excels in many AKC® events, including conformation as well as obedience, rally, and agility trials, where the breed can be seen succeeding at the most advanced levels. The English Springer's hunting ability on land and water is evaluated at AKC® spaniel hunting tests and field trials, both areas in which the breed demonstrates its superb acumen. The parent club hosts both an annual national specialty and field trial.

Intellectual property rights retained by Francie Nelson, Fanfare Springers, and donated to the American Kennel Club®/ESSFTA for this specific usage. No other use is permitted without written request.

Official Standard for the English Springer Spaniel

General Appearance: The English Springer Spaniel is a medium-sized sporting dog, with a compact body and a docked tail. His coat is moderately long, with feathering on his legs, ears, chest and brisket. His pendulous ears, soft gentle expression, sturdy build and friendly wagging tail proclaim him unmistakably a member of the ancient family of Spaniels. He is above all a well-proportioned dog, free from exaggeration, nicely balanced in every part. His carriage is proud and upstanding, body deep, legs strong and muscular, with enough length to carry him with ease. Taken as a whole, the English Springer Spaniel suggests power, endurance and agility. He looks the part of a dog that can go, and keep going, under difficult hunting conditions. At his best, he is endowed with style, symmetry, balance and enthusiasm, and is every inch a sporting dog of distinct spaniel character, combining beauty and utility.

Size, Proportion, Substance: The Springer is built to cover rough ground with agility and reasonable speed. His structure suggests the capacity for endurance. He is to be kept to medium size. Ideal height at the shoulder for dogs is 20 inches; for bitches, it is 19 inches. Those more than 1 inch under or over the breed ideal are to be faulted. A 20-inch dog, well-proportioned and in good condition, will weigh approximately 50 pounds; a 19-inch bitch will weigh approximately 40 pounds. The length of the body (measured from point of shoulder to point of buttocks) is slightly greater than the height at the withers. The dog too long in body, especially when long in the loin, tires easily and lacks the compact outline characteristic of the breed. A dog too short in body for the length of his legs, a condition which destroys balance and restricts gait, is equally undesirable. A Springer with correct substance appears well-knit and sturdy with good bone, however, he is never coarse or ponderous.

Head: The head is impressive without being heavy. Its beauty lies in a combination of strength and refinement. It is important that its size and proportion be in balance with the rest of the dog. Viewed in profile, the head appears approximately the same length as the neck and blends with the body in substance. The stop, eyebrows and chiseling of the bony structure around the eye sockets contribute to the Springer's beautiful and characteristic expression, which is alert, kindly and trusting. The eyes, more than any other feature, are the essence of the Springer's appeal. Correct size, shape, placement and color influence expression and attractiveness. The eyes are of medium size and oval in shape, set rather well-apart and fairly deep in their sockets. The color of the iris harmonizes with the color of the coat, preferably dark hazel in the liver and white dogs and black or deep brown in the black and white dogs. Eyerims are fully pigmented and match the coat in color. Lids are tight with little or no haw showing. Eyes that are small, round or protruding, as well as eyes that are yellow or brassy in color, are highly undesirable. Ears are long and fairly wide, hanging close to the cheeks with no tendency to stand up or out. The ear leather is thin and approximately long enough to reach the tip of the nose. Correct ear set is on a level with the eye and not too far back on the skull.

The skull is medium-length and fairly broad, flat on top and slightly rounded at the sides and back. The occiput bone is inconspicuous. As the skull rises from the foreface, it makes a stop, divided by a groove, or fluting, between the eyes. The groove disappears as it reaches the middle of the forehead. The amount of stop is moderate. It must not be a pronounced feature; rather it is a subtle rise where the muzzle joins the upper head. It is emphasized by the groove and by the position and shape of the eyebrows, which are well-developed. The muzzle is approximately the same length as the skull and one half the width of the skull. Viewed in profile, the toplines of the skull and muzzle lie in approximately parallel planes. The nasal bone is straight, with no inclination downward toward the tip of the nose, the latter giving an undesirable downfaced look. Neither is the nasal bone concave, resulting in a "dish-faced" profile; nor convex, giving the dog a Roman nose. The cheeks are flat, and the face is well-chiseled under the eyes. Jaws are of sufficient length to allow the dog to carry game easily: fairly square, lean and strong. The upper lips come down full and rather square to cover the line of the lower jaw, however, the lips are never pendulous or exaggerated. The nose is fully-pigmented, liver or black in color, depending on the color of the coat. The nostrils are well-opened and broad. Teeth are strong, clean, of good size and ideally meet in a close scissors bite. An even bite or one or two incisors slightly out of line are minor faults. Undershot, overshot and wry jaws are serious faults and are to be severely penalized.

Neck, Topline, Body: The neck is moderately long, muscular, clean and slightly arched at the crest. It blends gradually and smoothly into sloping shoulders. The portion of the topline from withers to tail is firm and slopes very gently. The body is short-coupled, strong and compact. The chest is deep, reaching the level of the elbows, with well-developed forechest; however, it is not so wide or round as to interfere with the action of the front legs. Ribs are fairly long, springing gradually to the middle of the body, then tapering as they approach the end of the ribbed section. The underline stays level with the elbows to a slight upcurve at the flank. The back is straight, strong and essentially level. Loins are strong, short and slightly arched. Hips are nicely rounded, blending smoothly into the hind legs. The croup slopes gently to the set of the tail, and tail-set follows the natural line of the croup. The tail is carried horizontally or slightly elevated and displays a characteristic lively, merry action, particularly when the dog is on game. A clamped tail (indicating timidity or undependable temperament) is to be faulted, as is a tail carried at a right angle to the backline in Terrier fashion.

Forequarters: Efficient movement in front calls for proper forequarter assembly. The shoulder blades are flat and fairly close together at the tips, molding smoothly into the contour of the body. Ideally, when measured from the top of the withers to the point of the shoulder to the elbow, the shoulder blade and upper arm are of apparent equal length, forming an angle of nearly 90 degrees; this sets the front legs well under the body and places the elbows directly beneath the tips of the shoulder blades. Elbows lie close to the body. Forelegs are straight with the same degree of size continuing to the foot. Bone is strong, slightly flattened, not too round or too heavy. Pasterns are short, strong and slightly sloping, with no suggestion of weakness. Dewclaws are usually removed. Feet are round or slightly oval. They are compact and well-arched, of medium size with thick pads, and well-feathered between the toes.

Hindquarters: The Springer should be worked and shown in hard, muscular condition with well-developed hips and thighs. His whole rear assembly suggests strength and driving power. Thighs are broad and muscular. Stifle joints are strong. For functional efficiency, the angulation of the hindquarter is never greater than that of the forequarter, and not appreciably less. The hock joints are somewhat rounded, not small and sharp in contour. Rear pasterns are short (about one-third the distance from the hip joint to the foot) and strong, with good bone. When viewed from behind,

the rear pasterns are parallel. Dewclaws are usually removed. The feet are the same as in front, except that they are smaller and often more compact.

Coat: The Springer has an outer coat and an undercoat. On the body, the outer coat is of medium length, flat or wavy, and is easily distinguishable from the undercoat, which is short, soft and dense. The quantity of undercoat is affected by climate and season. When in combination, outer coat and undercoat serve to make the dog substantially waterproof, weatherproof and thornproof. On ears, chest, legs and belly the Springer is nicely furnished with a fringe of feathering of moderate length and heaviness. On the head, front of the forelegs, and below the hock joints on the front of the hind legs, the hair is short and fine. The coat has the clean, glossy, "live" appearance indicative of good health. It is legitimate to trim about the head, ears, neck and feet, to remove dead undercoat, and to thin and shorten excess feathering as required to enhance a smart, functional appearance. The tail may be trimmed, or well fringed with wavy feathering. Above all, the appearance should be natural. Overtrimming, especially the body coat, or any chopped, barbered or artificial effect is to be penalized in the show ring, as is excessive feathering that destroys the clean outline desirable in a sporting dog. Correct quality and condition of coat is to take precedence over quantity of coat.

Color: All the following combinations of colors and markings are equally acceptable: (1) Black or liver with white markings or predominantly white with black or liver markings; (2) Blue or liver roan; (3) Tricolor: black and white or liver and white with tan markings, usually found on eyebrows, cheeks, inside of ears and under the tail. Any white portion of the coat may be flecked with ticking. Off colors such as lemon, red or orange are not to place.

Gait: The final test of the Springer's conformation and soundness is proper movement. Balance is a prerequisite to good movement. The front and rear assemblies must be equivalent in angulation and muscular development for the gait to be smooth and effortless. Shoulders which are well laid-back to permit a long stride are just as essential as the excellent rear quarters that provide driving power.

Seen from the side, the Springer exhibits a long, ground-covering stride and carries a firm back, with no tendency to dip, roach or roll from side to side. From the front, the legs swing forward in a free and easy manner. Elbows have free action from the shoulders, and the legs show no tendency to cross or interfere. From behind, the rear legs reach well under the body, following on a line with the forelegs. As speed increases, there is a natural tendency for the legs to converge toward a center line of travel. Movement faults include high-stepping, wasted motion; short, choppy stride; crabbing; and moving with the feet wide, the latter giving roll or swing to the body.

Temperament: The typical Springer is friendly, eager to please, quick to learn and willing to obey. Such traits are conducive to tractability, which is essential for appropriate handler control in the field. In the show ring, he should exhibit poise and attentiveness and permit himself to be examined by the judge without resentment or cringing. Aggression toward people and aggression toward other dogs is not in keeping with sporting dog character and purpose and is not acceptable. Excessive timidity, with due allowance for puppies and novice exhibits, is to be equally penalized.

Summary: In evaluating the English Springer Spaniel, the overall picture is a primary consideration. One should look for *type*, which includes general appearance and outline, and also for *soundness*, which includes movement and temperament. Inasmuch as the dog with a smooth easy gait must be reasonably sound and well-balanced, he is to be highly regarded, however, not to the extent of forgiving him for not looking like an English Springer Spaniel. An atypical dog, too short or long in leg length or foreign in head or expression, may move well, but he is not to be preferred over a good all-round specimen that has a minor fault in movement. It must be remembered that the English Springer Spaniel is first and foremost a sporting dog of the Spaniel family, and he must *look*, *behave* and *move* in character.

Approved February 12, 1994
Effective March 31, 1994

Meet the Field Spaniel

Recognized by AKC® in 1878
Field Spaniel Society of America (fieldspaniels.org), formed in 1978

Traits
- Sweet
- Family Dog
- Sensitive

HISTORY

The Field Spaniel came to the United States a couple of decades prior to the establishment of the American Kennel Club in 1884. A Field Spaniel named Benedict won his championship at the Westminster Kennel Club show in 1883. Two years later, Dash (AKC® number 3126) became the first Field Spaniel registered by the American Kennel Club® in 1885. Like so many breeds, the Field Spaniel nearly died out during World War II, and by 1942, the breed had disappeared from AKC® lists. Dick Squier and Carl Tuttle imported English dogs in 1967, reintroducing the breed to America. All of today's dogs descend from the four British dogs surviving after World War II.

As the breed's popularity increased, the Field Spaniel Society of America was formed in 1978. While the breed is on solid footing today, it still ranks in the bottom fifth in AKC® registrations.

FORM AND FUNCTION

Early Field Spaniels went through several phases influenced by a new interest in dog shows. For a time, they were long, low, and heavy. Most were black. A series of crosses with Springers and Cockers eliminated the early exaggerations, producing today's dog—a substantial, well-boned dog able to hunt in dense cover, with moderate coat and a readily recognizable sculpted head. The Field Spaniel is slightly longer than tall, with a short loin, well-sprung rib cage, and plenty of endurance for a full day's work in the field.

LIVING WITH A FIELD

Although he excels in many roles today—agility performer, tracking dog, hunter—given the choice, the playful, enthusiastic Field Spaniel would probably choose "family dog" as his favorite job. Fields love to be near their people, whether this activity involves hiking, swimming, or watching the game on TV.

People who love Field Spaniels are a diverse group. The dogs are equally content in an apartment or farm, with a young, active family or an older owner. Today, the dogs are recognized as handsome, versatile companions. The joke among owners is that "you can't have just one."

Puppy buyers should ask their breeder to select a puppy whose temperament is a match to their lifestyle. Fields are reserved by nature, so positive training is most effective, and constant exposure to new people and experiences is helpful for socialization.

The breeder will be happy to show new owners the way to groom their new family member. Unless the dog will be shown, a daily brushing to minimize shedding, weekly or biweekly nail trimmings, and monthly trimming of feet and clipping of the throat and upper ears are all the grooming required.

Young puppies should be exercised with care until their growth plates close at about eighteen months. Free play is best for developing bones. Once the pup matures, he will be happy to accompany his owner jogging, biking, or hiking. Dogs can begin swimming or hunt training at any age.

COMPETITION

Once you become the owner of a Field Spaniel, a world of AKC® activities opens to you. Field Spaniels earn titles in conformation, agility, obedience, tracking, and spaniel hunting tests. Many are certified therapy dogs, while others use their exceptional noses to detect bombs or contraband. And in their off time, all are happy on the family-room couch.

Official Standard for the Field Spaniel

General Appearance: The Field Spaniel is a combination of beauty and utility. It is a well balanced, substantial hunter-companion of medium size, built for activity and endurance in a heavy cover and water. It has a noble carriage; a proud but docile attitude; is sound and free moving. Symmetry, gait, attitude and purpose are more important than any one part.

Size, Proportion, Substance: Balance between these three components is essential. *Size*—Ideal height for mature adults at the withers is 18 inches for dogs and 17 inches for bitches. A one inch deviation either way is acceptable. *Proportion*—A well balanced dog, somewhat longer than tall. The ratio of length to height is approximately 7:6. (Length is measured on a level from the foremost point of the shoulder to the rearmost point of the buttocks.) *Substance*—Solidly built, with moderate bone, and firm smooth muscles.

Head: Conveys the impression of high breeding, character and nobility, and must be in proportion to the size of the dog. *Expression*—Grave, gentle and intelligent. *Eyes*—Almond in shape, open and of medium size; set moderately wide and deep. Color: dark hazel to dark brown. The lids are tight and show no haw; rims comparable to nose in color. *Ears*—Moderately long (reaching the end of the muzzle) and wide. Set on slightly below eye level: pendulous, hanging close to the head; rolled and well feathered. Leather is moderately heavy, supple, and rounded at the tip. *Skull*—The crown is slightly wider at the back than at the brow and lightly arched laterally; sides and cheeks are straight and clean. The occiput is distinct and rounded. Brows are slightly raised. The stop is moderate, but well defined by the brows. The face is chiseled beneath the eyes. *Muzzle*—Strong, long and lean, neither snipy nor squarely cut. The nasal bone is straight and slightly divergent from parallel, sloping downward toward the nose from the plane of the top skull. In profile, the lower plane curves gradually from the nose to the throat. Jaws are level. *Nose*—Large, flesh and well developed with open nostrils. Set on as an extension of the muzzle. Color: solid: light to dark brown or black as befits the color of the coat. *Lips*—Close fitting, clean, and sufficiently deep to cover the lower jaw without being

pendulous. *Bite*—Scissors or level, with complete dentition. Scissors preferred.

Neck, Topline, Body: *Neck*—Long, strong, muscular, slightly arched, clean, and well set into shoulders. *Topline*—The neck slopes smoothly into the withers; the back is level, well muscled, firm and strong; the croup is short and gently rounded. *Body*—The prosternum is prominent and well fleshed. The depth of chest is roughly equal to the length of the front leg from elbow to ground. The rib cage is long and extending into a short loin. Ribs are oval, well sprung and curve gently into a firm loin. *Loin*— Short, strong, and deep, with little or no tuck up. *Tail*—Set on low, in line with the croup, just below the level of the back with a natural downward inclination. Docked tails preferred, natural tails are allowed. The tail whether docked or natural length should be in balance with the overall dog.

Forequarters: Shoulders blades are oblique and sloping. The upper arm is closed-set; elbows are directly below the withers, and turn neither in nor out. Bone is flat. Forelegs are straight and well boned to the feet. Pasterns are moderately sloping but strong. Dewclaws may be removed. Feet face forward and are large, rounded, and webbed, with strong, well arched relatively tight toes and thick pads.

Hindquarters: Strong and driving; stifles and hocks only moderately bent. Hocks well let down; pasterns relatively short, strong and parallel when viewed from the rear. Hips moderately broad and muscular; upper thigh broad and powerful; second thigh well muscled. Bone corresponds to that of the forelegs. No dewclaws.

Coat: Single; moderately long; flat or slightly wavy; silky; and glossy; dense and water repellent. Moderate setter-like feathering adorns the chest, underbody, backs of the legs, buttocks, and may also be present on the second thigh and underside of the tail. Pasterns have clean outlines to the ground. There is short, soft hair between the toes. Overabundance of coat, or cottony texture,

AKC Official Guide to Sporting Dogs

impractical for field work should be penalized. Trimming is limited to that which enhances the natural appearance of the dog. Amount of coat or absence of coat should not be faulted as much as structural faults.

Color: Black, liver, golden liver or shades thereof, in any intensity (dark or light); either self- colored or bi-colored. Bi-colored dogs must be roaned and/or ticked in white areas. Tan points are acceptable on the aforementioned colors and are the same as any normally tan pointed breed. White is allowed on the throat, chest, and/or brisket, and may be clear, ticked, or roaned on a self-color dog. The sable pattern, a lighter undercoat with darker shading as tipping or dark overlay, with or without a mask present, is a disqualification. Disqualifications: The sable pattern, a lighter undercoat with darker shading as tipping or dark overlay, with or without a mask present.

Gait: The head is carried alertly, neither so high nor so low as to impede motion or stride. There is good forward reach that begins in the shoulder, coupled with strong drive from the rear, giving the characteristic effortless, long, low majestic stride. When viewed from front and/or rear elbows and hocks move parallel. The legs move straight, with slight convergence at increased speed. When moving, the tail is carried inclined slightly downward or level with the back, and with a wagging motion. Tail carried above the back is incorrect. Side movement is straight and clean, without energy wasting motions. Overreaching and single tracking are incorrect. The Field Spaniel should be shown at its own natural speed in an endurance trot, preferably on a loose lead, in order to evaluate its movement.

Temperament: Unusually docile, sensitive, fun-loving, independent and intelligent, with a great affinity for human companionship. They may be somewhat reserved in initial meetings. Any display of shyness, fear, or aggression is to be severely penalized.

Disqualifications: *The sable pattern, a lighter undercoat with darker shading as tipping or dark overlay, with or without a mask present.*

Approved April 6, 2020
Effective June 30, 2020

Meet the Flat-Coated Retriever

Recognized by AKC® in 1915
Flat-Coated Retriever Society of America (fcrsa.org), formed in 1960

Traits
- Responsive
- Happy
- Loving

HISTORY

As humankind became more adept at hunting winged game, and at greater distances, the use of dogs to assist in finding and retrieving game grew in importance. Any such dog with these skills was considered a retriever, regardless of appearance or type. In Britain in the early nineteenth century, by selective breeding and crossbreeding to perfect this skill, the retriever proper came into existence.

At the same time, dogs with retrieving abilities were traveling back and forth between Britain and Newfoundland, where a retriever most often referred to as the St. John's Newfoundland was developed. This dog, likely of British ancestry, contributed to the creation of the Wavy-Coated (and subsequently to the Flat-Coated) Retriever.

The greatest credit for the integration of these retrievers into a stable breed in the late 1800s goes to S. E. Shirley, who also was the founder of The Kennel Club (Britain). The breed gained enormous popularity as numerous important fanciers strove to refine the quality, elegance, and working abilities of the Flat-Coated Retriever. Most notable among these was H. R. Cooke, who kept Flat-Coats in his renowned Riverside kennel for more than seventy years.

The two World Wars took a heavy toll on the numbers of the breed, and after World War II, it was not easy to pick up the threads of disappearing lines. Stanley O'Neill, one of the greatest authorities on the breed, worked tirelessly to put the breed on as sound a footing as possible.

In the decades since, the popularity of the Flat-Coated Retriever has continued to increase. The parent club in the United States is the Flat-Coated Retriever Society of America, which held its first national specialty in 1978. Although Flat-Coats are not as popular as many other AKC® breeds, the breed's enthusiastic supporters make the Flat-Coated Retriever national specialties among the most heavily attended of any breed.

Flat-Coated Retriever

FORM AND FUNCTION

The beauty and elegance of the Flat-Coated Retriever must also be balanced with soundness and a willingness to please, such that he can do a day's work as a retriever. He is a versatile family companion and hunting retriever with a happy and active demeanor, intelligent expression, and clean lines. The coat is thick and flat-lying, and the legs and tail are well-feathered. A proud carriage, responsive attitude, waving tail, and overall look of functional strength, quality, style and symmetry complete the picture of the typical Flat-Coat.

LIVING WITH A FLAT-COAT

Character is a primary and outstanding asset of the Flat-Coat. He is a happy, responsive, loving dog who expects and deserves to be a member of the family. He needs regular exercise and occasional grooming. He is a versatile working dog, multi-talented, sensible, bright, and tractable. In training and competition, the Flat-Coat demonstrates stability and a desire to please with a confident, optimistic, and outgoing attitude characterized by a wagging tail. He also has a sense of whimsy and is known as the Peter Pan of the dog world.

If you think a Flat-Coated Retriever would be a great addition to your family, begin your search by talking to several breeders. A responsible breeder should be willing to advise and mentor you, exercises great care in the placement of puppies, and makes a lifelong commitment to the well-being of the Flat-Coated Retrievers he or she produces.

COMPETITION

Besides being an excellent family companion, a Flat-Coat can participate in many fun and exciting activities. Flat-Coated Retrievers do well in a variety of retrieving events and as personal hunting companions. They also excel in activities such as conformation, obedience, agility, and tracking.

Official Standard for the Flat-Coated Retriever

General Appearance: The Flat-Coated Retriever is a versatile family companion hunting retriever with a happy and active demeanor, intelligent expression, and clean lines. The Flat-Coat has been traditionally described as showing *"power without lumber and raciness without weediness."*

The distinctive and most important features of the Flat-Coat are the silhouette (both moving and standing), smooth effortless movement, head type, coat and character. In silhouette the Flat-Coat has a long, strong, clean, "one piece" head, which is unique to the breed. Free from exaggeration of stop or cheek, the head is set well into a moderately long neck which flows smoothly into well laid back shoulders. A level topline combined with a deep, long rib cage tapering to a moderate tuck-up create the impression of a blunted triangle. The brisket is well developed and the forechest forms a prominent prow. This utilitarian retriever is well balanced, strong, but elegant; never cobby, short legged or rangy. The coat is thick and flat lying, and the legs and tail are well feathered. A proud carriage, responsive attitude, waving tail and overall look of functional strength, quality, style and symmetry complete the picture of the typical Flat-Coat.

Judging the Flat-Coat moving freely on a loose lead and standing naturally is more important than judging him posed. Honorable scars should not count against the dog.

Size, Proportion, Substance: *Size*—Individuals varying more than an inch either way from the preferred height should be considered not practical for the types of work for which the Flat-Coat was developed. Preferred height is 23 to 24½ inches at the withers for dogs, 22 to 23½ inches for bitches. Since the Flat-Coat is a working hunting retriever he should be shown in lean, hard condition, free of excess weight. *Proportion*—The Flat-Coat is not cobby in build. The length of the body from the point of the shoulder to the rearmost projection of the upper thigh is slightly more than the height at the withers. The female may be slightly longer to better accommodate the carrying of puppies. *Substance*—Moderate. Medium bone is flat or oval rather than round; strong but never massive, coarse, weedy or fine. This applies throughout the dog.

Head: The long, clean, well molded head is adequate in size and strength to retrieve a large pheasant, duck or hare with ease. *Skull and muzzle*—The impression of the skull and muzzle being "cast in one piece" is created by the fairly flat skull of moderate breadth and flat, clean cheeks, combined with the long, strong, deep muzzle which is well filled in before, between and beneath the eyes. Viewed from above, the muzzle is nearly equal in length and breadth to the skull. *Stop*—There is a gradual, slight, barely perceptible stop, avoiding a down or dish-faced appearance. Brows are slightly raised and mobile, giving life to the expression. Stop must be evaluated in profile so that it will not be confused with the raised brow. *Occiput* not accentuated, the skull forming a gentle curve where it fits well into the neck. *Expression* alert, intelligent and kind. *Eyes* are set widely apart. Medium sized, almond shaped, dark brown or hazel; not large, round or yellow. Eye rims are self-colored and tight. *Ears* relatively small, well set on, lying close to the side of the head and thickly feathered. Not low set (houndlike or setterish). *Nose*—Large open nostrils. Black on black dogs, brown on liver dogs. *Lips* fairly tight, firm, clean and dry to minimize the retention of feathers. *Jaws* long and strong, capable of carrying a hare or a pheasant. *Bite*—Scissors bite preferred, level bite acceptable. Broken teeth should not count against the dog. *Severe faults:* Wry and undershot or overshot bites with a noticeable gap must be severely penalized.

Neck, Topline, Body: *Neck* strong and slightly arched for retrieving strength. Moderately long to allow for easy seeking of the trail. Free from throatiness. Coat on neck is untrimmed. *Topline* strong and level. *Body*—*Chest (Brisket)*—Deep, reaching to the elbow and only moderately broad. *Forechest*—Prow prominent and well developed. *Rib cage* deep, showing good length from forechest to last rib (to allow ample space for all body organs), and only moderately broad. The foreribs fairly flat showing a gradual spring, well arched in the center of the body but rather lighter towards the loin. *Underline*—Deep chest tapering to a moderate *tuck-up*. *Loin* strong, well muscled and long enough to allow for agility, freedom of movement and length of stride, but never weak or loosely coupled. *Croup* slopes very slightly; rump moderately broad and well muscled. *Tail* fairly straight, well set on, with bone reaching approximately to the hock joint. When the dog is in motion, the tail is carried happily but without curl as a smooth extension of the topline, never much above the level of the back.

Forequarters: *Shoulders* long, well laid back shoulder blade with *upper arm* of approximately equal length to allow for efficient reach. Musculature wiry rather than bulky. *Elbows* clean, close to the body and set well back under the withers. *Forelegs* straight and strong with medium bone of good quality. *Pasterns* slightly sloping and strong. *Dewclaws*—Removal of dewclaws is optional. *Feet* oval or round.

Medium sized and tight with well arched toes and thick pads.

Hindquarters: Powerful with angulation in balance with the front assembly. *Upper thighs* powerful and well muscled. *Stifle*—Good turn of stifle with sound, strong joint. *Second thighs* (Stifle to hock joint)—Second or lower thigh as long as or only slightly longer than upper thigh. *Hock*—Hock joint strong, well let down. *Dewclaws* There are no hind dewclaws. *Feet* oval or round. Medium sized and tight with well arched toes and thick pads.

Coat: Coat is of moderate length density and fullness, with a high lustre. The ideal coat is straight and flat lying. A slight waviness is permissible but the coat is not curly, wooly, short, silky or fluffy. The Flat-Coat is a working retriever and the coat must provide protection from all types of weather, water and ground cover. This requires a coat of sufficient texture, length and fullness to allow for adequate insulation. When the dog is in full coat the ears, front, chest, back of forelegs, thighs and underside of tail are thickly feathered without being bushy, stringy or silky. Mane of longer heavier coat on the neck extending over the withers and shoulders is considered typical, especially in the male dog, and can cause the neck to appear thicker and the withers higher, sometimes causing the appearance of a dip behind the withers. Since the Flat-Coat is a hunting retriever, the feathering is not excessively long. *Trimming*—The Flat-Coat is shown with as natural a coat as possible and must not be penalized for lack of trimming, as long as the coat is clean and well brushed. Tidying of ears, feet, underline and tip of tail is acceptable. Whiskers serve a specific function and it is preferred that they not be trimmed. Shaving or barbering of the head, neck or body coat must be severely penalized.

Color: Solid black or solid liver. *Disqualification*—Yellow, cream or any color other than black or liver.

Gait: Sound, efficient movement is of critical importance to a hunting retriever. The Flat-Coat viewed from the side covers ground efficiently and movement appears balanced, free flowing and well coordinated, never choppy, mincing or ponderous. Front and rear legs reach well forward and extend well back, achieving long clean strides. Topline appears level, strong and supple while dog is in motion.

Summary: The Flat-Coat is a strong but elegant, cheerful hunting retriever. Quality of structure, balance and harmony of all parts both standing and in motion are essential. As a breed whose purpose is of a utilitarian nature, structure, condition and attitude should give every indication of being suited for hard work.

Temperament: Character is a primary and outstanding asset of the Flat-Coat. He is a responsive, loving member of the family, a versatile working dog, multi-talented, sensible, bright and tractable. In competition the Flat-Coat demonstrates *stability* and a desire to please with a confident, happy and outgoing attitude characterized by a wagging tail. Nervous, hyperactive, apathetic, shy or obstinate behavior is undesirable. *Severe fault*—Unprovoked aggressive behavior toward people or animals is *totally* unacceptable.

Character: Character is as important to the evaluation of stock by a potential breeder as any other aspect of the breed standard. The Flat-Coat is primarily a family companion hunting retriever. He is keen and birdy, flushing within gun range, as well as a determined, resourceful retriever on land and water. He has a great desire to hunt with self-reliance and an uncanny ability to adapt to changing circumstances on a variety of upland game and waterfowl.

As a family companion he is sensible, alert and highly intelligent; a lighthearted, affectionate and adaptable friend. He retains these qualities as well as his youthfully good-humored outlook on life into old age. The adult Flat-Coat is usually an adequate alarm dog to give warning, but is a good-natured, optimistic dog, basically inclined to be friendly to all.

The Flat-Coat is a cheerful, devoted companion who requires and appreciates living with and interacting as a member of his family. To reach full potential in any endeavor he absolutely must have a strong personal bond and affectionate individual attention.

Disqualification: *Yellow, cream or any color other than black or liver.*

Approved September 11, 1990
Effective October 30, 1990

Meet the German Shorthaired Pointer

Recognized by AKC® in 1930
German Shorthaired Pointer Club of America (gspca.org), formed in 1938

Traits
- Energetic
- Intelligent
- Willing to Please

HISTORY

In 1861, German hunters set out to create their own national breed of shorthaired pointing dog. They wanted an all-purpose gun dog who would respond to any kind of work in the field, woods, and water, capable of being used for all game, large or small, furred or feathered. Highly prized were the abilities to naturally point, retrieve, and track with little training. This gun dog would also be a companion who would live in the home and interact with the family. Early German Shorthairs were derived from the old German pointer, Hannover Hound, and early pointer stock from Italy, France, and the Mediterranean area of Spain.

Dr. Charles R. Thornton of Missoula, Montana, is credited with the first import in 1925, from Edward Rindt of Austria. Bred prior to shipping, Senta v. Hohenbruck whelped a litter of seven on July 4, 1925.

Two World Wars took a toll on the German breeding stock, but from 1930 to 1950, Shorthairs arrived in the United States with German immigrants and returning soldiers. By 1970, it had become one of the most popular hunting dogs in North and South America as well as in large portions of Europe.

FORM AND FUNCTION

Medium size, standing over a lot of ground, balanced front to rear, graceful outline, clean head, sloping shoulders, deep chest, short powerful back, strong quarters, good bone and muscle tone, taut coat, and well-carried tail—these are the attributes of a versatile all-purpose gun dog capable of high performance in both the field and water. As such, the GSP may be required to cover all types of uneven terrain, manage obstacles, go into heavy brush, or navigate through

AKC Official Guide to Sporting Dogs

water. Because German Shorthairs were bred to perform under these circumstances, their size, agile movement, and quick foot speed lent themselves to other types of performance competition. The short back allows for quick energy transfer and, combined with the medium size, means the dog can work longer without tiring. The deep chest as opposed to a wide one allows the dog to slip easily through heavy brush or glide through the water with little resistance. The taut coat will not get caught in the brush, pick up stickers, or hold mud and ice formation.

LIVING WITH A GSP

This is not a breed for a person with a sedentary lifestyle, and one size doesn't necessarily fit all when it comes to finding the perfect companion pet, show prospect, or performance dog. The best owner will understand the prey drive of a hunting breed. If not used as a hunting companion, a GSP will need someone with an active lifestyle to redirect and match his high energy level. Early training is essential: this is an intelligent breed that learns quickly via observation and/or consistent training sessions. GSPs need a purpose, and without one, they can be quite destructive if left to their own devices. They can be extremely challenging from six months to three years old.

COMPETITION

Athletic and biddable, GSPs excel in all canine sports. Today, the GSP knows no peers when it comes to range, scenting capabilities, staunch point, and recognition of frequent bird cover. Dominating both retrieving and non-retrieving stakes in the AKC® Pointing Breed Gun Dog Championships since its inception in 1994, the breed ranks second among the sporting breeds with more than 250 Dual Champions. GSPs are eligible to compete in pointing-breed field trials and hunting tests. They also compete in conformation, companion events, and the coursing ability test. GSPs make wonderful therapy dogs.

Official Standard for the German Shorthaired Pointer

General Appearance: The German Shorthaired Pointer is a versatile hunter, an all-purpose gun dog capable of high performance in field and water. The judgment of Shorthairs in the show ring reflects this basic characteristic. The overall picture which is created in the observer's eye is that of an aristocratic, well balanced, symmetrical animal with conformation indicating power, endurance and agility and a look of intelligence and animation. The dog is neither unduly small nor conspicuously large. It gives the impression of medium size, but is like the proper hunter, "with a short back, but standing over plenty of ground." Symmetry and field quality are most essential. A dog in hard and lean field condition is not to be penalized; however, overly fat or poorly muscled dogs are to be penalized. A dog well balanced in all points is preferable to one with outstanding good qualities and defects. Grace of outline, clean-cut head, sloping shoulders, deep chest, powerful back, strong quarters, good bone composition, adequate muscle, well carried tail and taut coat produce a look of nobility and indicate a heritage of purposefully conducted breeding. Further evidence of this heritage is movement which is balanced, alertly coordinated and without wasted motion.

Size, Proportion, Substance: *Size*—height of dogs, measured at the withers, 23 to 25 inches. Height of bitches, measured at the withers, 21 to 23 inches. Deviations of one inch above or below the described heights are to be severely penalized. Weight of dogs 55 to 70 pounds. Weight of bitches 45 to 60 pounds. *Proportion*—measuring from the forechest to the rearmost projection of the rump and from the withers to the ground, the Shorthair is permissibly

German Shorthaired Pointer

either square or slightly longer than he is tall. *Substance*—thin and fine bones are by no means desirable in a dog which must possess strength and be able to work over any type of terrain. The main importance is not laid so much on the size of bone, but rather on the bone being in proper proportion to the body. Bone structure too heavy or too light is a fault. Tall and leggy dogs, dogs which are ponderous because of excess substance, doggy bitches, and bitchy dogs are to be faulted.

Head: The *head* is clean-cut, is neither too light nor too heavy, and is in proper proportion to the body. The *eyes* are of medium size, full of intelligence and expression, good-humored and yet radiating energy, neither protruding nor sunken. The eye is almond shaped, not circular. The preferred color is dark brown. Light yellow eyes are not desirable and are a fault. Closely set eyes are to be faulted. China or wall eyes are to be disqualified. The *ears* are broad and set fairly high, lie flat and never hang away from the head. Their placement is just above eye level. The ears laid in front without being pulled, should extend to the corner of the mouth. In the case of heavier dogs, the ears are correspondingly longer. Ears too long or fleshy are to be faulted. The *skull* is reasonably broad, arched on the side and slightly round on top. Unlike the Pointer, the median line between the eyes at the forehead is not too deep and the occipital bone is not very conspicuous. The foreface rises gradually from nose to forehead. The rise is more strongly pronounced in the dog than in the bitch. The jaw is powerful and the muscles well developed. The line to the forehead rises gradually and never has a definite stop as that of the Pointer, but rather a stop-effect when viewed from the side, due to the position of the eyebrows. The *muzzle* is sufficiently long to enable the dog to seize game properly and be able to carry it for a long time. A pointed muzzle is not desirable. The depth is in the right proportion to the length, both in the muzzle and in the skull proper. The length of the muzzle should equal the length of the skull. A dish-shaped muzzle is a fault. A definite Pointer stop is a serious fault. Too many wrinkles in the forehead is a fault.

AKC Official Guide to Sporting Dogs

The nose is brown on a liver dog and black on a black dog. The larger the nose the better and nostrils should be well opened and broad. A spotted nose is not desirable. A flesh colored nose disqualifies. The chops fall away from the somewhat projecting nose. Lips are full and deep yet are never flewy. The teeth are strong and healthy. The molars intermesh properly. The *bite* is a true scissors bite. A perfect level bite is not desirable and must be penalized. Extreme overshot or undershot disqualifies.

Neck, Topline, Body: The *neck* is of proper length to permit the jaws reaching game to be retrieved, sloping downwards on beautifully curving lines. The nape is rather muscular, becoming gradually larger toward the shoulders. Moderate throatiness is permitted. The skin is close and tight. The chest in general gives the impression of depth rather than breadth; for all that, it is in correct proportion to the other parts of the body. The chest reaches down to the elbows, the ribs forming the thorax show a rib spring and are not flat or slabsided; they are not perfectly round or barrel-shaped. The back ribs reach well down. The circumference of the thorax immediately behind the elbows is smaller than that of the thorax about a hand's breadth behind elbows, so that the upper arm has room for movement. Tuck-up is apparent. The back is short, strong, and straight with a slight rise from the root of the tail to the withers. The loin is strong, is of moderate length, and is slightly arched. An excessively long, roached or swayed back must be penalized. The hips are broad with hip sockets wide apart and fall slightly toward the tail in a graceful curve. A steep croup is a fault. The *tail* is set high and firm, and must be docked, leaving approximately 40 percent of its length. The tail hangs down when the dog is quiet and is help horizontally when he is walking. The tail must never be curved over the back toward the head when the dog is moving. A tail curved or bent toward the head is to be severely penalized.

Forequarters: The shoulders are sloping, movable, and well covered with muscle. The shoulder blades lie flat and are well laid back nearing a 45 degree angle. The upper arm (the bones between the shoulder and the elbow joint) is as long as possible, standing away somewhat from the trunk so that the straight and closely muscled legs, when viewed from the front, appear to be parallel. Elbows which stand away from the body or are too close result in toes turning inwards or outwards and must be faulted. Pasterns are strong, short and nearly vertical with a slight spring. Loose, short-bladed or straight shoulders must be faulted. Knuckling over is to be faulted. Dewclaws on the forelegs may be removed. The feet are compact, close-knit and round to spoon-shaped. The toes are sufficiently arched and heavily nailed. The pads are strong, hard and thick.

Hindquarters: Thighs are strong and well muscled. Stifles are well bent. Hock joints are well angulated and strong with straight bone structure from hock to pad. Angulation of both stifle and hock joint is such as to achieve the optimal balance of drive and traction. Hocks turn neither in nor out. Cowhocked legs are a serious fault.

Coat: The hair is short and thick and feels tough to the hand; it is somewhat longer on the underside of the tail and the back edges of the haunches. The hair is softer, thinner and shorter on the ears and the head. Any dog with long hair in the body coat is to be severely penalized.

Color: The coat may be of solid liver or a combination of liver and white such as liver and white ticked, liver patched and white ticked, or liver roan. Or the coast may be of solid black or any combination of black and white such as black and white ticked, black patched and white ticked, or black roan. Any other color or color combination is a disqualification. A dog with any area of red, orange, lemon or tan, or a dog solid white will be disqualified.

Gait: A smooth lithe gait is essential. It is to be noted that as gait increases from the walk to a faster speed, the legs converge beneath the body. The tendency to single track is desirable. The forelegs reach well ahead as if to pull in the ground without giving the appearance of a hackney gait. The hindquarters drive the back legs smoothly and with great power.

Temperament: The Shorthair is friendly, intelligent, and willing to please. The first impression is that of a keen enthusiasm for work without indication of nervous or flighty character.

Disqualifications: *China or wall eyes. Flesh colored nose. Extreme overshot or undershot. Any color combination of colors other than liver or black as described in the standard. A dog with any area of red, orange, lemon or tan or a dog solid white.*

Approved October 11, 2022
Effective January 1, 2023

Meet the German Wirehaired Pointer

Recognized by AKC® in 1959
German Wirehaired Pointer Club of America (gwpca.com), formed in 1959

Traits
- Intelligent
- Eager
- Affectionate

HISTORY

German Wirehaired Pointers trace their origins back to the late 1800s in Germany. Breeders wanted to develop a rugged, versatile hunting dog who would work closely with either one person or a small party of people hunting on foot over varied terrain—from the mountainous regions of the Alps, to dense forests, to more open areas around farms and small towns. The breed the Germans desired had to have a coat that would protect the dog when working in heavy cover or in cold water yet be easy to maintain. The goal was to develop a wire-coated, medium-sized dog that could search for, locate, and point upland game; work both feather and fur with equal skill; retrieve waterfowl; be a close-working, easily trained gun dog; be able to track and locate wounded game; be fearless when hunting "sharp" game such as fox; be a devoted companion and pet; and be a watchdog for his owner's family and property.

In 1959, the German Wirehaired Pointer Club of America was established and the breed was recognized by the American Kennel Club®.

Wirehairs today have many roles. They are excellent dogs for the everyday hunter who, much like the Germans of more than a century ago, wants a dog who can literally do it all. It is not uncommon for hunters and their Wirehairs to jump-hunt ducks in the morning; hunt quail, pheasant, or chukar in the afternoon; and wait in a blind for an evening flight of geese. Wirehairs serve as companions who would rather sleep on their owners' feet than anywhere else.

FORM AND FUNCTION

When observing a group of GWPs, keep in mind the jobs they are asked to perform: they must have strength in their movement and be athletic to allow them to cover uneven ground for hours on end; the skin should be tight to the body to resist tearing in thick woods and briars; their coat should be long, harsh, and dense enough to shed water but not so long as to collect burrs, sticks, mud, and ice. The eye should not be saggy to allow seeds to accumulate. Their temperament should be brave and upstanding, unafraid, but not aggressive.

LIVING WITH A WIREHAIR

Along with its intelligence and will, the breed also has the capability to be very creative and somewhat independent. Wirehairs generally are a high-energy, high-drive, although not hyper, breed. A job is a must. GWPs are extremely devoted dogs. They crave human companionship, doing best in a home where they are permitted a very close relationship with their people.

Young GWPs are typically fun-loving and playful. With proper supervision for both children and dog, GWPs and kids do very well together. As with any dog, very young children should be taught to properly handle a puppy and to understand the difference between playing with a dog and hurting it. The breed's high prey drive may not make it the best choice for families with cats and other small animals.

The GWPCA recommends that owners who are looking for a GWP puppy as a hunting companion watch the sire and/or dam working in the field, if at all possible. Talk to the breeder and inform him or her of the type of work you will expect the dog to do, the type of environment he will live in, and the activity level of your household.

COMPETITION

GWPs compete successfully in conformation shows, pointing-breed field trials and hunting tests, agility, obedience, and many other performance and companion events. They also serve individuals and communities in the form of therapy dogs, assistance dogs, drug-detection dogs, search and rescue dogs, and much more.

Official Standard for the German Wirehaired Pointer

General Appearance: The German Wirehaired Pointer is a well muscled, medium sized dog of distinctive appearance. Balanced in size and sturdily built, the breed's most distinguishing characteristics are its weather resistant, wire-like coat and its facial furnishings. Typically Pointer in character and style, the German Wirehaired Pointer is an intelligent, energetic and determined hunter.

Size, Proportion, Substance: The *height* of males should be from 24 to 26 inches at the withers. Bitches are smaller but not under 22 inches. To insure the working quality of the breed is maintained, dogs that are either over or under the specified height must be severely penalized. The body is a little longer than it is high, as 10 is to 9. The German Wirehaired Pointer is a versatile hunter built for agility and endurance in the field. Correct size and balance are essential to high performance.

Head: The head is moderately long. *Eyes* are brown, medium in size, oval in contour, bright and clear and overhung with medium length eyebrows. Yellow eyes are not desirable. The *ears* are rounded but not too broad and hang close to the head. The *skull* broad and the occipital bone not too prominent. The *stop* is medium. The *muzzle* is fairly long with nasal bone straight, broad and parallel to the top of the skull. The *nose* is dark brown with nostrils wide open. A spotted or flesh colored nose is to be penalized. The *lips* are a trifle pendulous but close to the jaw and bearded. The *jaws* are strong with a full complement of evenly set and properly intermeshing teeth. The incisors meet in a true *scissors bite*.

Neck, Topline, Body: The *neck* is of medium length, slightly arched and devoid of dewlap. The entire *back line* showing a perceptible slope down from withers to croup. The skin throughout is notably tight to the body. The *chest* is deep and capacious with ribs

German Wirehaired Pointer

well sprung. The *tuck-up* apparent. The back is short, straight and strong. Loins are taut and slender. Hips are broad with the croup nicely rounded. The *tail* is set high, carried at or above the horizontal when the dog is alert. The tail is docked to approximately two-fifths of its original length.

Forequarters: The shoulders are well laid back. The forelegs are straight with elbows close. Leg bones are flat rather than round, and strong, but not so heavy or coarse as to militate against the dog's natural agility. Dewclaws are generally removed. Round in outline, the feet are webbed, high arched with toes close, pads thick and hard, and nails strong and quite heavy.

Hindquarters: The angles of the hindquarters balances that of the forequarters. A straight line drawn vertically from the buttock (ischium) to the ground should land just in front of the rear foot. The *thighs* are strong and muscular. The *hind legs* are parallel when viewed from the rear. The *hocks* (metatarsus) are short, straight and parallel turning neither in nor out. Dewclaws are generally removed. Feet as in forequarters.

Coat: The functional wiry coat is the breed's most distinctive feature. A dog must have a correct coat to be of correct type. The coat is weather resistant and, to some extent, water-repellent. The undercoat is dense enough in winter to insulate against the cold but is so thin in summer as to be almost invisible. The distinctive outer coat is straight, harsh, wiry and flat lying, and is from 1 to 2 inches in length. The outer coat is long enough to protect against the punishment of rough cover, but not so long as to hide the outline of the dog. On the lower legs the coat is shorter and between the toes it is of softer texture. On the skull the coat is naturally short and close fitting. Over the shoulders and around the tail it is very dense and heavy. The tail is nicely coated, particularly on the underside, but devoid of feather. Eyebrows are of strong, straight hair. Beard and whiskers are medium length. The hairs in the liver patches of a

German Wirehaired Pointer

liver and white dog may be shorter than the white hairs. A short smooth coat, a soft woolly coat, or an excessively long coat is to be severely penalized. While maintaining a harsh, wiry texture, the puppy coat may be shorter than that of an adult coat. Coats may be neatly groomed to present a dog natural in appearance. Extreme and excessive grooming to present a dog artificial in appearance should be severely penalized.

Color: The coat is liver and white, usually either liver and white spotted, liver roan, liver and white spotted with ticking and roaning or solid liver. The head is liver, sometimes with a white blaze. The ears are liver. Any black in the coat is to be severely penalized.

Gait: The dog should be evaluated at a moderate gait. Seen from the side, the movement is free and smooth with good reach in the forequarters and good driving power in the hindquarters. The dog carries a firm back and exhibits a long, ground-covering stride. When moving in a straight line the legs swing forward in a free and easy manner and show no tendency to cross or interfere. There should be no signs of elbowing out. The rear legs follow on a line with the forelegs. As speed increases, the legs will converge toward a center line of travel.

Temperament: Of sound, reliable temperament, the German Wirehaired Pointer is at times aloof but not unfriendly toward strangers; a loyal and affectionate companion who is eager to please and enthusiastic to learn.

Approved October 10, 2006
Effective January 1, 2007

Meet the Golden Retriever

Recognized by AKC® in 1925
Golden Retriever Club of America (grca.org), formed in 1938

Traits
- Friendly
- Reliable
- Devoted

HISTORY

From the rocky and heather-clad hillsides of Scotland came the athletic, moderately made Golden Retriever with his distinctive golden coat. In nineteenth-century Scotland and England, the pursuit of game birds was not merely sport but also important in supplying meat for the table. The advent of the breech-loading shotgun brought with it a need for efficient retrieving dogs, and various of the landed gentry developed distinctive strains of retrievers.

All the British retrievers share much common ancestry, chiefly the old Wavy-Coated Retriever, itself developed largely from the St. John's Dog or Lesser Newfoundland, combined with British spaniels and setters. The origins of the Golden Retriever are well documented. Best known is the record of Lord Tweedmouth's line, descended from "Nous," the only yellow in a litter of black Wavy-Coats born in 1864. Two litters by Nous, bred with a Tweed Water Spaniel named "Belle," started the Tweedmouth line, blended with another Tweed Water Spaniel, a red setter, and a few black Wavy- or Flat-Coated Retrievers.

The American Kennel Club® first registered Goldens in 1925. Imports, of course, were the foundation of the breed in North America. Their success as working gun dogs and as companions soon spread through the Central Flyway of the United States and to both the East and West Coasts. By the late 1930s, Goldens were participating quite successfully in bench shows and field trials. While a relatively uncommon breed for decades, by the 1970s the Golden's rise in popularity was strong and steady, and Goldens have been in the top ten of all breeds annually since 1976.

FORM AND FUNCTION

Careful selection produced a strain of useful yellow-coated working retrievers for both fur and feathered game. Good temperament was essential, for these

AKC Official Guide to Sporting Dogs

dogs were required to work closely both with people and alongside other dogs. The water-resistant double coat, with its protective undercoat, is an important characteristic. The Golden can be found in shades from very pale to deep red-gold, often with lighter shadings on underparts and feathering. The Golden's structure is without any sort of exaggeration, suitable for prolonged work over rugged terrain in an equally rugged climate. He has the leg length for galloping and climbing, the strength and suppleness for agility in heavy cover. His equable temperament and high degree of willingness let him work in varied circumstances. This is the sort of dog the breed standard describes.

LIVING WITH A GOLDEN

While the Golden can be an admirable companion, he is also an active, athletic canine who needs regular exercise, attention, and training, especially in the puppy and teenage stages. Many Golden owners help satisfy these demands (and have fun!) with participation in training classes and events such as obedience and rally, hunting tests, tracking, and agility. Conformation shows can be fun, and the really dedicated may get hooked on field trials. Goldens also have excelled as search and rescue dogs, scenting specialists, assistance dogs, guide dogs for the blind, and, of course, as practical, companionable gun dogs. The same qualities that make the Golden so useful in its original work also fit the breed for these modern uses. A Golden may not be the dog for the compulsively tidy—he can shed profusely (frequent diligent brushing helps considerably). Although the Golden loves mud and water in any form, owners find that a correct Golden coat is practical and easily maintained. As retrievers, Goldens have a strong compulsion to "fetch and carry": every Golden needs toys to learn proper retrieving, or he'll carry anything available—shoes, gloves, even throw rugs or sofa pillows!

The best source for a Golden Retriever puppy is a responsible breeder who will be able to supply information on the parents, temperament, working aptitude, and the results of the usual examinations. Good breeders always want the best homes for their puppies; buyers should not be surprised if the breeder has as many questions for them as they do for the breeder. But the good breeder will always be there for support and even to take back or help rehome the dog if need be.

COMPETITION

Goldens are highly versatile and excel in all kinds of dog sports. They are standouts in obedience, rally, and agility, as well as retriever hunting tests and field trials. Goldens are among the most versatile of breeds, performing some of the most vital services in today's world, including therapy, guiding the blind and other assistance work, scenting, and search and rescue.

Official Standard for the Golden Retriever

General Appearance: A symmetrical, powerful, active dog, sound and well put together, not clumsy nor long in the leg, displaying a kindly expression and possessing a personality that is eager, alert and self-confident. Primarily a hunting dog, he should be shown in hard working condition. Overall appearance, balance, gait and purpose to be given more emphasis than any of his component parts. *Faults*—Any departure from the described ideal shall be considered faulty to the degree to which it interferes with the breed's purpose or is contrary to breed character.

Size, Proportion, Substance: Males 23 to 24 inches in height at withers; females 21½ to 22½ inches. Dogs up to 1 inch above or below standard size should be proportionately penalized. Deviation in height of more than 1 inch from the standard shall *disqualify*. Length from breastbone to point of buttocks slightly greater than height at withers in ratio of 12:11. Weight for dogs 65 to 75 pounds; bitches 55 to 65 pounds.

Head: Broad in skull, slightly arched laterally and longitudinally without prominence of frontal bones (forehead) or occipital bones. *Stop* well defined but not abrupt. *Foreface* deep and wide, nearly as long as skull. *Muzzle* straight in profile, blending smooth and strongly into skull; when viewed in profile or from above, slightly deeper and wider at stop than at tip. No heaviness in flews. Removal of whiskers is permitted but not preferred. *Eyes* friendly and intelligent in expression, medium large with dark, close-fitting rims, set well apart and reasonably deep in sockets. Color preferably dark brown; medium brown acceptable. Slant eyes and narrow, triangular eyes detract from correct expression and are to be faulted. No white or haw visible when looking straight ahead. Dogs showing evidence of functional abnormality of eyelids or eyelashes (such as, but not limited to, trichiasis, entropion, ectropion, or distichiasis) are to be excused from the ring. *Ears* rather short with front edge attached well behind and just above the eye and falling close to cheek. When pulled forward, tip of ear should just cover the eye. Low, hound-like ear set to be faulted. *Nose* black or brownish black, though fading to a lighter shade in cold weather not serious. Pink nose or one seriously lacking in pigmentation to be faulted. *Teeth* scissors bite, in which the outer side of the lower incisors touches the inner side of the upper incisors. Undershot or overshot bite is a *disqualification*. Misalignment of teeth (irregular placement of incisors) or a level bite (incisors meet each other edge to edge) is undesirable, but not to be confused with undershot or overshot. Full dentition. Obvious gaps are serious faults.

Neck, Topline, Body: *Neck* medium long, merging gradually into well laid back shoulders, giving sturdy, muscular appearance. No throatiness.

Backline strong and level from withers to slightly sloping croup, whether standing or moving. Sloping backline, roach or sway back, flat or steep croup to be faulted. *Body* well balanced, short coupled, deep through the chest. *Chest* between forelegs at least as wide as a man's closed hand including thumb, with well developed forechest. Brisket extends to elbow. *Ribs* long and well sprung but not barrel shaped, extending well towards hindquarters. *Loin* short, muscular, wide and deep, with very little tuck-up. Slab-sidedness, narrow chest, lack of depth in brisket, excessive tuck-up to be faulted. *Tail* well set on, thick and muscular at the base, following the natural line of the croup. Tail bones extend to, but not below, the point of hock. Carried with merry action, level or with some moderate upward curve; never curled over back nor between legs.

Forequarters: Muscular, well coordinated with hindquarters and capable of free movement. *Shoulder blades* long and well laid back with upper tips fairly close together at withers. *Upper arms* appear about the same length as the blades, setting the elbows back beneath the upper tip of the blades, close to the ribs without looseness. *Legs,* viewed from the front, straight with good bone, but not to the point of coarseness. *Pasterns* short and strong, sloping slightly with no suggestion of weakness. Dewclaws on forelegs may be removed, but are normally left on. *Feet* medium size, round, compact, and well knuckled, with thick pads. Excess hair may be trimmed to show natural size and contour. Splayed or hare feet to be faulted.

Hindquarters: Broad and strongly muscled. Profile of croup slopes slightly; the pelvic bone slopes at a slightly greater angle (approximately 30 degrees from horizontal). In a natural stance, the femur joins the pelvis at approximately a 90-degree angle; *stifles* well bent; *hocks* well let down with short, strong *rear pasterns. Feet* as in front. *Legs* straight when viewed from rear. Cow-hocks, spread hocks, and sickle hocks to be faulted.

Coat: Dense and water-repellent with good undercoat. Outer coat firm and resilient, neither coarse nor silky, lying close to body; may be straight or wavy. Untrimmed natural ruff; moderate feathering on back of forelegs and on underbody; heavier feathering on front of neck, back of thighs and underside of tail. Coat on head, paws, and front of legs is short and even. Excessive length, open coats, and limp, soft coats are very undesirable. Feet may be trimmed and stray hairs neatened, but the natural appearance of coat or outline should not be altered by cutting or clipping.

Color: Rich, lustrous golden of various shades. Feathering may be lighter than rest of coat. With the exception of graying or whitening of face or body due to age, any white marking, other than a few white hairs on the chest, should be penalized according to its extent. Allowable light shadings are not to be confused with white markings. Predominant body color which is either extremely pale or extremely dark is undesirable. Some latitude should be given to the light puppy whose coloring shows promise of deepening with maturity. Any noticeable area of black or other off-color hair is a serious fault.

Gait: When trotting, gait is free, smooth, powerful and well coordinated, showing good reach. Viewed from any position, legs turn neither in nor out, nor do feet cross or interfere with each other. As speed increases, feet tend to converge toward center line of balance. It is recommended that dogs be shown on a loose lead to reflect true gait.

Temperament: Friendly, reliable, and trustworthy. Quarrelsomeness or hostility towards other dogs or people in normal situations, or an unwarranted show of timidity or nervousness, is not in keeping with Golden Retriever character. Such actions should be penalized according to their significance.

Disqualifications: *Deviation in height of more than 1 inch from standard either way. Undershot or overshot bite.*

Approved October 13, 1981
Reformatted August 18, 1990

Meet the Gordon Setter

Recognized by AKC® in 1884
Gordon Setter Club of America (gsca.org), formed in 1924

Traits
- Affectionate
- Alert
- Confident

HISTORY

Beauty, brains, and bird sense are the outstanding qualities of the handsome black and tan setter from Scotland whose lineage dates back to at least 1620, when Markham, a writer of the time, praised the "black and fallow setting dog" as "hardest to endure labor." Popular among Scottish hunters for decades, the black and tan setter came into prominence in the kennels of the Fourth Duke of Gordon in the late 1820s. Commenting on these kennels, a writer familiar with the Duke's Gordons described them much as a sportsman would describe a Gordon Setter of today: "The Castle Gordon Setters are as a rule easy to break and naturally back well. They are not fast dogs but they have good staying powers and can keep on steadily from morning until night. Their noses are first-class and they seldom make a false point on what is called at field trials a sensational stand. ... When they stand you may be sure there are birds."

Attracted as much by the Gordon Setter's beauty as by his superior hunting ability, George Blunt imported a pair, Rake and Rachel, from Castle Gordon to America in 1842. Rachel was subsequently given to the American statesman, Daniel Webster. In later years, importations from Great Britain and the Scandinavian countries helped to perfect the American strains and lead the Gordon to achieve great popularity. The Gordon Setter was one of nine original breeds recognized by the AKC® at its founding in 1884.

FORM AND FUNCTION

This breed, the heaviest of the setters, is built for long days in the field, with plenty of bone and substance. He should also have a smooth, free gait. The dark coloring makes him highly visible, so he can be spotted easily in snow or in light fields. The Gordon's characteristic eagerness to work for a loving master has never changed over the centuries, nor has his keen intellect and retentive memory; he improves with age, with no need for retraining each season. Gordon breeders, backed by a strong national club, make

no distinction between field or show types in their standard for the breed.

LIVING WITH A GORDON

The quality that endears the Gordon both to the pet owner and the sportsman is his devoted loyalty to members of the household. Suspicious of the unwanted intruder, the Gordon is not the pal of every passerby, but he lives for the pleasure of being near his owners. This almost fanatical devotion has helped make the Gordon not only a responsive gun dog but also a mannerly, eager-to-please dog in the home. Slow to mature, a Gordon is a pup into his middle years, retaining his stamina and function well into old age. Training, using positive reinforcement, is very important for a young Gordon, giving him guidance and structure. While strenuous exercise is not a requirement, Gordons (and their families) are happiest when they have adequate exercise. They are known as "great talkers" and develop a large and amusing vocabulary of sounds to express themselves. A moderate amount of coat care is necessary to keep a Gordon in good shape. Gordons should be bathed at least every two to three weeks, brushed daily, and groomed regularly.

Buying a puppy through a reputable AKC® breeder is a must. The Gordon Setter Club of America maintains a list of members in good standing who have puppies available or plan to breed. A good breeder will evaluate the prospective home and match the home to the right dog. Gordon Setter breeders and owners have been diligent to improve health in the breed; they work constantly to maintain type without compromising health. The lifespan of a Gordon averages ten to twelve years, with many living well into their teens.

COMPETITION

Gordons are intelligent and do well in conformation, obedience, agility, tracking, rally, pointing-breed field trials, and hunting tests. They remain cherished hunting companions as well. Many Gordons have successfully performed as therapy dogs.

Official Standard for the Gordon Setter

General Appearance: The Gordon Setter is a good-sized, sturdily built, black and tan dog, well muscled, with plenty of bone and substance, but active, upstanding and stylish, appearing capable of doing a full day's work in the field. He has a strong, rather short back, with well sprung ribs and a short tail. The head is fairly heavy and finely chiseled. His bearing is intelligent, noble, and dignified, showing no signs of shyness or viciousness. Clear colors and straight or slightly waved coat are correct. He suggests strength and stamina rather than extreme speed. Symmetry and quality are most essential. A dog well balanced in all points is preferable to one with outstanding good qualities and defects. A smooth, free movement, with high head carriage, is typical.

Size, Proportion, Substance: *Size*—Shoulder height for males, 24 to 27 inches; females, 23 to 26 inches. Weight for males, 55 to 80 pounds; females, 45 to 70 pounds. Animals that appear to be over or under the prescribed weight limits are to be judged on the basis of conformation and condition. Extremely thin or fat dogs are discouraged on the basis that under or overweight hampers the true working ability of the Gordon Setter. The weight-to-height ratio makes him heavier than other Setters. *Proportion*—The distance from the forechest to the back of the thigh is approximately equal the height from the ground to the withers. The Gordon Setter has plenty of bone and substance.

Head: Head deep, rather than broad, with plenty of brain room. *Eyes* of fair size, neither too deep-set nor too bulging, dark brown, bright and wise. The shape is oval rather than round. The lids are tight. *Ears* set low on the head approximately on line with the eyes, fairly large and thin, well folded and carried close to the head. *Skull* nicely rounded, good-sized, broadest between the ears. Below and above the eyes is lean and the cheeks as narrow as the leanness of the head allows. The head should have a clearly indicated stop. *Muzzle* fairly long and not pointed, either as seen from above or from the side. The flews are not pendulous. The muzzle is the same length as the skull from occiput to stop and the top of the muzzle is parallel to the line of the skull extended. *Nose* broad, with open nostrils and black in color. The lip line from the nose to the flews shows a sharp, well-defined, square contour. *Teeth* strong and white, meeting in front in a scissors bite, with the upper incisors slightly forward of the lower incisors. A level bite is not a fault. Pitted teeth from distemper or allied infections are not penalized.

Neck, Topline, Body: *Neck* long, lean, arched to the head, and without throatiness. *Topline* moderately sloping. *Body* short from shoulder to hips. Chest deep and not too broad in front; the ribs well sprung, leaving plenty of lung room. The chest reaches to the elbows. A pronounced forechest is in evidence. Loins short and broad and not arched. Croup nearly flat, with only a slight slope to the tailhead. *Tail* short and not reaching below the hocks, carried horizontal or nearly so, not docked, thick at the root and finishing in a fine point. The placement of the tail is important for correct carriage. When the angle of the tail bends too sharply at the first coccygeal bone, the tail will be carried too gaily or will droop. The tail placement is judged in relationship to the structure of the croup.

Forequarters: Shoulders fine at the points, and laying well back. The tops of the shoulder blades are close together. When viewed from behind, the neck appears to fit into the shoulders in smooth, flat lines that gradually widen from neck to shoulder. The angle formed by the shoulder blade and upper arm bone is approximately 90 degrees when the dog is standing so that the foreleg is perpendicular to the ground. Forelegs big-boned, straight and not bowed, with elbows free and not turned in or out. Pasterns are strong, short and nearly vertical with a slight

Gordon Setter

AKC Official Guide to Sporting Dogs

spring. Dewclaws may be removed. Feet catlike in shape, formed by close-knit, well arched toes with plenty of hair between; with full toe pads and deep heel cushions. Feet are not turned in or out.

Hindquarters: The hind legs from hip to hock are long, flat and muscular; from hock to heel, short and strong. The stifle and hock joints are well bent and not turned either in or out. When the dog is standing with the rear pastern perpendicular to the ground, the thighbone hangs downward parallel to an imaginary line drawn upward from the hock. Feet as in front.

Coat: Soft and shining, straight or slightly waved, but not curly, with long hair on ears, under stomach and on chest, on back of the fore and hind legs, and on the tail. The feather which starts near the root of the tail is slightly waved or straight, having a triangular appearance, growing shorter uniformly toward the end.

Color and Markings: Black with tan markings, either of rich chestnut or mahogany color. Black pencilling is allowed on the toes. The borderline between black and tan colors is clearly defined. There are not any tan hairs mixed in the black. The tan markings are located as follows: (1) Two clear spots over the eyes and not over three-quarters of an inch in diameter; (2) On the sides of the muzzle. The tan does not reach to the top of the muzzle, but resembles a stripe around the end of the muzzle from one side to the other; (3) On the throat; (4) Two large clear spots on the chest; (5) On the inside of the hind legs showing down the front of the stifle and broadening out to the outside of the hind legs from the hock to the toes. It must not completely eliminate the black on the back of the hind legs; (6) On the forelegs from the carpus, or a little above, downward to the toes; (7) Around the vent; (8) A white spot on the chest is allowed, but the smaller the better. Predominantly tan, red or buff dogs which do not have the typical pattern of markings of a Gordon Setter are ineligible for showing and undesirable for breeding. Predominantly tan, red or buff dogs are ineligible for showing and undesirable for breeding.

Scale of Points	
To be used as a guide when judging the Gordon Setter:	
Head and neck (include ears and eyes)	10
Body	15
Shoulders, forelegs, forefeet	10
Hind legs and feet	10
Tail	5
Coat	8
Color and markings	5
Temperament	10
Size, general appearance	15
Gait	12
Total	**100**

Gait: A bold, strong, driving free-swinging gait. The head is carried up and the tail "flags" constantly while the dog is in motion. When viewed from the front, the forefeet move up and down in straight lines so that the shoulder, elbow and pastern joints are approximately in line. When viewed from the rear, the hock, stifle and hip joints are approximately in line. Thus the dog moves in a straight pattern forward without throwing the feet in or out. When viewed from the side, the forefeet are seen to lift up and reach forward to compensate for the driving hindquarters. The hindquarters reach well forward and stretch far back, enabling the stride to be long and the drive powerful. The overall appearance of the moving dog is one of smooth-flowing, well balanced rhythm, in which the action is pleasing to the eye, effortless, economical and harmonious.

Temperament: The Gordon Setter is alert, gay, interested, and confident. He is fearless and willing, intelligent and capable. He is loyal and affectionate, and strong-minded enough to stand the rigors of training.

Disqualification: *Predominantly tan, red or buff dogs.*

Approved October 7, 2002
Effective November 27, 2002

Meet the Irish Red and White Setter

Recognized by AKC® in 2009
Irish Red and White Setter Association of America
(www.irishredwhitesetterassociation.com), formed in 1997

Traits
- Energetic
- Friendly
- Determined

HISTORY

The Irish Red and White Setter dates back to the eighteenth century and is the progenitor of the Irish Red Setter, which appeared in the late nineteenth century. The origins are unknown and any specific origin claims are speculative at best. Historical images show the dogs pointing birds in a low crouch, or set, ostensibly allowing the hunter to throw a net past the dog and capture the prey. Irish Red and Whites remained popular among sportsmen in the United States up to the 1920s. Between the 1920s and 1950s, the breed fell out of favor, and breeding was continued only in Ireland and that on a limited basis. Resurrection of the breed started in the mid-twentieth century, and specimens were reintroduced to the United States in the 1980s.

FORM AND FUNCTION

The Irish Red and White Setter is bred to hunt for upland game. As the name suggests, the breed finds birds and sets or points, then holds for the hunter to flush. To this end, the dog is bred for stamina, independence, and confidence in the field. The dog is of moderate size: dogs are 24½ to 26 inches tall; bitches are 22½ to 24 inches tall, with moderate bone, relative to their size. This combination provides the foundation for a dog who can hunt for hours on end without tiring. Because the dog is a hunting

companion, he must have a pleasant disposition and work well with other dogs. The demeanor of the breed makes it an attractive choice for active families. Males tend to be more affectionate than females.

LIVING WITH AN IRISH RED AND WHITE

The Irish Red and White Setter is first and foremost a hunting dog with a naturally high energy level that must be accommodated. These stunningly beautiful sporting dogs, with their striking red and white coats, are courageous, spirited, and determined. They can be delightful companions. When a family decides on an Irish Red and White Setter, it is essential to interview breeders, carefully observe the disposition of the sire and dam, and inquire about genetic screening. The ideal owner for the breed offers the opportunity for plenty of exercise and attention. The breed requires a minimum amount of grooming. Attention must be paid to cleaning the ears, keeping toenails trimmed, and combing the coat on a weekly basis. Basic obedience training will make the dog easier to live with and will teach him to respect his status within his family. Training should be under the direction of an experienced trainer. Avoid trainers who use harsh methods; the breed does not respond well in these situations.

COMPETITION

Irish Red and White Setters are eligible to compete in pointing-breed field trials, hunting tests, conformation, obedience, agility, and tracking.

Official Standard for the Irish Red and White Setter

General Appearance: The Irish Red and White Setter is bred primarily for the field. The standard as set out hereunder must be interpreted chiefly from this point of view and all Judges at Bench Shows must be encouraged to judge the exhibits chiefly from the working standpoint. The appearance is strong and powerful, well balanced and proportioned without lumber; athletic rather than racy with an aristocratic, keen and intelligent attitude.

Size, Proportion & Substance: Dogs are 24½ to 26 inches tall; bitches are 22½ to 24 inches tall. The length of body from point of shoulder to point of buttock is equal or longer than height to top of withers, up to a ratio of 10 L-9 H. Bone is moderate in proportion to size.

Head: *Expression*—The gentle expression displays a kindly, friendly attitude. The *eyes* are dark hazel or dark brown; round or nearly round, with slight prominence and tightly fitted eyelids. The *ears* are set level with the eyes, well back, lying close to the head. *Skull*—The skull is broad, in proportion to the body and rounded without showing an occipital protuberance. *Stop*—The stop is distinct, but not exaggerated. *Muzzle*—The muzzle is clean and square, of equal length to skull, with parallel planes. *Bite*—A scissors bite is ideal; a level bite is acceptable.

Neck, Topline & Body: *Neck*—The neck is moderately long, very muscular, but not too thick, slightly arched, free from all tendency to throatiness. *Topline*—The topline of the dog, from the withers to the croup should be level, not sloping. The croup should be well rounded and sloping slightly downward to the tailset.

Body—The body is strong & muscular with a deep chest and well sprung ribs. The back is very muscular and powerful. *Tail*—The tail is of moderate length, not reaching below the hock, strong at the root, tapering to fine point; no appearance of ropiness and carried level with or below the back.

Forequarters: Angulation—shoulder blade well laid back with upper arm equal in length and forming a nearly right angle with the shoulder blade. Tips of shoulder blades meeting fairly close, lie flat and are smooth with contours of body. Elbow—The elbows are free, turning neither in nor out. Legs—The forelegs are straight and sinewy, well boned, with strong pasterns. Feet—The feet are close-knit with plenty of feathering between toes.

Hindquarters: The hindquarters are wide and powerful. Legs—The legs are of strong bone, well muscled and sinewy. The thighs, from hip to hock, are long and muscular. The stifle is well bent. The hock is well let down and turns neither in nor out, hocks are of moderate length and strong. Feet—The feet are close-knit with plenty of feathering between toes.

Coat: Long silky fine hair called "Feathering" is present on the back of the fore and hind legs and on the outer ear flap, also a reasonable amount is on the flank extending onto the chest and throat forming a fringe. All feathering is straight, flat and not overly profuse. The tail is well feathered. On the head, front of legs and other parts of the body the hair is short, flat and free from curl but a slight wave is permissible.

Color: The base color is white with solid red patches (clear islands of red color); both colors show the maximum of life and bloom. Flecking but not roaning is permitted around the face and feet and up the foreleg as far as the elbow and up the hind leg as far as the hock. Roaning, flecking and mottling on any other part of the body is objectionable.

Gait: When moving at the trot, the gait is long striding, very lively, graceful and efficient. The head is held high, and the hindquarters drive smoothly and with great power. The forelegs reach well ahead and remain low. Seen from front or rear, the forelegs and hind legs below the hock joint move perpendicularly to the ground with no crossing or weaving.

Grooming: The trimming of an Irish Red and White Setter should be kept to a minimum, maintaining a neat natural appearance and not to be shaved with clippers. Light trimming with thinning shears is allowed. Under the ears, tail, pasterns and hocks may be trimmed for neatness. Feet may be cleared of hair including the bottom and around the edges leaving hair between the toes. No other trimming is allowed including the whiskers which shall remain intact.

Temperament: They display a kindly, friendly attitude, behind which is discernible determination, courage and high spirit.

Faults: Any departure from the foregoing standard is considered a fault and the seriousness of the fault is in exact proportion to its degree.

Approved July 9, 2019
Effective October 1, 2019

Meet the Irish Setter

Recognized by AKC® in 1878
Irish Setter Club of America (irishsetterclub.org), formed in 1891

Traits
- Outgoing
- Sweet-Natured
- Active

HISTORY

The Irish Setter, as its name implies, has its origins in the soft, rolling fields of Ireland. It is uncertain which breeds make up the original Irish Setter, but the speculation is that it comes down from the land spaniels of Spain, with the possible inclusion of the Pointer and the Irish Water Spaniel. Whatever the original crosses, by the early 1800s, the Irish Setter was a good-sized solid red dog, as depicted in paintings and on tapestries alongside his fellow English and Gordon Setters, and looking very much like the Irish of today. The dog was popular with the gentry and respected as a good hunter—many families bred their own strain. With the advent of dog shows in England and Ireland in the mid-1850s, the Irish Setter became a winner in both the show ring and the field.

In the United States, the Irish Setter reached its peak of popularity in the mid-1970s when the movie *Big Red* hit the theaters. This, coupled with the fact that President Nixon had an Irish in the White House, made these beautiful red dogs a fairly common sight. Approximately 70,000 Irish were born during the mid-1970s; far more than serious breeders wanted. Today, approximately 2,000 are registered each year with the AKC®, and there can be a wait to get your puppy.

FORM AND FUNCTION

While the Irish Setter is versatile, his purpose is that of an aristocratic bird dog. He is swift in the field, and his structure is one of a dog who can do a full day of hunting. The level planes of his head allow for excellent scenting, and his length and depth of muzzle make it perfect for carrying upland game, both big and small. The long neck enhances his ability to retrieve game from the ground without constant crouching. The overall frame and bone of the Irish Setter are neither coarse nor heavy, as heaviness would make running arduous over the open, often soft and bog-like land in Ireland.

LIVING WITH AN IRISH SETTER

When looking for a puppy, remember that the cute red ball of fur will grow to be approximately 26 to 28 inches high, and weigh somewhere between 65 and 80 pounds. The breed's standard calls for a "rollicking personality," so be prepared for some Irish antics; this temperament is a part of the charm of the breed. When starting your search for a puppy, refer to the Irish Setter Club of America website for the online breeders list and scan the website for all pertinent information regarding the breed. All puppies should be sold with a contract, stating specifics, from the breeder.

Irish Setters require good exercise and moderate grooming. Correct exercise is imperative for the conditioning and mental well-being of these canine athletes and can come in the form of free running, leash walking, or jogging when age appropriate. The silky coat of the Irish can easily tangle, but good consistent brushing easily manages the coat, and the occasional trip to a groomer for a proper grooming will keep your dog looking at his peak.

COMPETITION

The Irish Setter is a versatile breed and excels at many events. Apart from conformation and pointing breed field trials and hunting tests, the Irish makes an excellent obedience dog, is very successful in agility, and is seen at the end of the leash of many winning Junior Handlers. As a breed, they are loyal and loving companions with an outgoing personality that make them, upon maturity, a joy to live with and compete with.

Official Standard for the Irish Setter

General Appearance: The Irish Setter is an active, aristocratic bird dog, rich red in color, substantial yet elegant in build. Standing over 2 feet tall at the shoulder, the dog has a straight, fine, glossy coat, longer on ears, chest, tail and back of legs. Afield, the Irish Setter is a swift-moving hunter; at home, a sweet natured, trainable companion.

Irish Setter

At their best, the lines of the Irish Setter so satisfy in overall balance that artists have termed it the most beautiful of all dogs. The correct specimen always exhibits balance, whether standing or in motion. Each part of the dog flows and fits smoothly into its neighboring parts without calling attention to itself.

Size, Proportion, Substance: There is no disqualification as to size. The make and fit of all parts and their overall balance in the animal are rated more important. 27 inches at the withers and a show weight of about 70 pounds is considered ideal for the dog; the bitch 25 inches, 60 pounds. Variance beyond an inch up or down is to be discouraged. *Proportion*—Measuring from the breastbone to rear of thigh and from the top of the withers to the ground, the Irish Setter is slightly longer than it is tall. *Substance*—All legs sturdy with plenty of bone. Structure in the male reflects masculinity without coarseness. Bitches appear feminine without being slight of bone.

Head: Long and lean, its length at least double the width between the ears. Beauty of head is emphasized by delicate chiseling along the muzzle, around and below the eyes, and along the cheeks. *Expression* soft, yet alert. *Eyes* somewhat almond shaped, of medium size, placed rather well apart, neither deep set nor bulging. Color, dark to medium brown. *Ears* set well back and low, not above level of eye. Leather thin, hanging in a neat fold close to the head, and nearly long enough to reach the nose. The *skull* is oval when viewed from above or front; very slightly domed when viewed in profile. The brow is raised, showing a distinct stop midway between the tip of the nose and the well-defined occiput (rear point of skull). Thus the nearly level line from occiput to brow is set a little above, and parallel to, the straight and equal line from eye to nose. *Muzzle* moderately deep, jaws of nearly equal length, the underline of the jaws being almost parallel with the top line of the muzzle. *Nose* black or chocolate; nostrils wide. Upper lips fairly square but not pendulous. The *teeth* meet in a scissors bite in which the upper incisors fit closely over the lower, or they may meet evenly.

Neck, Topline, Body: *Neck* moderately long, strong but not thick, and slightly arched; free from throatiness and fitting smoothly into the shoulders. *Topline* of body from withers to tail should be firm and incline slightly downward without sharp drop at the croup. The *tail* is set on nearly level with the croup as a natural extension of the topline, strong at root, tapering to a fine point, nearly long enough to reach the hock. Carriage straight or curving slightly upward, nearly level with the back. *Body* sufficiently long to permit a straight and free stride. *Chest* deep, reaching approximately to the elbows with moderate forechest, extending beyond the point where the shoulder joins the upper arm. Chest is of moderate width so that it does not interfere with forward motion and extends rearwards to well sprung ribs. *Loins* firm, muscular and of moderate length.

Forequarters: Shoulder blades long, wide, sloping well back, fairly close together at the withers. Upper arm and shoulder blades are approximately the same length, and are joined at sufficient angle to bring the elbows rearward along the brisket in line with the top of the withers. The elbows moving freely incline neither in nor out. *Forelegs* straight and sinewy. Strong, nearly straight pastern. *Feet* rather small, very firm, toes arched and close.

Hindquarters: Hindquarters should be wide and powerful with broad, well developed thighs. Hind legs long and muscular from hip to hock; short and perpendicular from hock to ground; well angulated at stifle and hock joints, which, like the elbows, incline neither in nor out. Feet as in front.

Angulation of the forequarters and hindquarters should be balanced.

Coat: Short and fine on head and forelegs. On all other parts of moderate length and flat. Feathering long and silky on ears; on back of forelegs and thighs long and fine, with a pleasing fringe of hair on belly and brisket extending onto the chest. Fringe on tail moderately long and tapering. All coat and feathering as straight and free as possible from curl or wave. The Irish Setter is trimmed for the show ring to emphasize the lean head and clean neck. The top third of the ears and the throat nearly to the breastbone are trimmed. Excess feathering is removed to show the natural outline of the foot. All trimming is done to preserve the natural appearance of the dog.

Color: Mahogany or rich chestnut red with no black. A small amount of white on chest, throat or toes, or a narrow centered streak on skull is not to be penalized.

Gait: At the trot the gait is big, very lively, graceful and efficient. At an extended trot the head reaches slightly forward, keeping the dog in balance. The forelegs reach well ahead as if to pull in the ground without giving the appearance of a hackney gait. The hindquarters drive smoothly and with great power. Seen from front or rear, the forelegs, as well as the hind legs below the hock joint, move perpendicularly to the ground, with some tendency towards a single track as speed increases. Structural characteristics which interfere with a straight, true stride are to be penalized.

Temperament: The Irish Setter has a rollicking personality. Shyness, hostility or timidity are uncharacteristic of the breed. An outgoing, stable temperament is the essence of the Irish Setter.

Approved August 14, 1990
Effective September 30, 1990

Meet the Irish Water Spaniel

Recognized by AKC® in 1884
Irish Water Spaniel Club of America (iwsca.org), formed in 1937

Traits
- Intelligent
- Hardworking
- Brave

HISTORY

In Ireland in the 1830s, Dublin sportsman Justin McCarthy wanted a powerful and loyal bird-hunting partner. He is credited with breeding the first pure-type Irish Water Spaniel: sturdy enough for upland retrieving and courageous enough to plunge into icy Irish bogs—a handsome, wickedly smart, and fun-loving companion with a bold, dashing temperament. McCarthy's celebrated "Boatswain" is considered to be the ancestor of the IWS we know today.

IWS popularity soared, and by 1875, the breed was the third most popular sporting dog in the United States. It was one of the original nine breeds recognized by the AKC® in 1884. Today, the IWS is considered a rare breed; fewer than 150 puppies are born per year in the United States.

FORM AND FUNCTION

An Irish Water Spaniel has immediately identifiable, unforgettable characteristics that make a truly unique dog—a curly liver brown coat of longish ringlets of hair; a topknot of long, loose curls; a smooth, shorthaired muzzle; a beard growing at the base of the throat; and a "rat tail" of very short smooth hair, except for short curls at the base.

Often considered a dual-purpose hunting dog, the IWS successfully retrieves upland game as well as waterfowl. The excellent vision and marking abilities of the IWS, combined with a keen nose, protective coat, soft mouth, and tenacious attitude, make him a truly wonderful hunting companion. The IWS is first and foremost a retriever and is classified as such by the AKC®, but it may also earn AKC® titles in spaniel hunt tests.

LIVING WITH AN IRISH WATER SPANIEL

The Irish Water Spaniel's endearing sense of humor has earned it the title of "Clown of the Sporting Group." Although IWS antics can be quite amusing, this highly intelligent breed quickly learns behaviors that please people and bring rewards in the form of positive human interaction. The IWS excels as a close member of an active family. This is not a breed to be relegated to the backyard. An IWS needs a significant amount of daily human interaction to stay emotionally healthy.

As with all breeds, to develop appropriate social behaviors, it is important to provide the IWS with early and continuing socialization and training. Although exuberantly demonstrative with those whom they know, these dogs can be reserved with strangers. An IWS responds best to positive, motivational training methods (food, toys, praise) not a heavy-handed disciplinary approach.

He requires regular grooming and care to maintain a healthy coat, ears, teeth, and nails. A thorough combing is generally needed every two to four weeks and bathing every month or so. The coat may be cut short for easier maintenance. Contrary to popular myth, the IWS does shed, although far less than most breeds. Although no dog is truly "hypoallergenic," many people allergic to dogs live comfortably with an IWS.

COMPETITION

The Irish Water Spaniel has stayed true to McCarthy's vision as a versatile dog with great success in the show ring and various performance and companion events. The IWS is eligible to compete in AKC® spaniel hunting tests as well as in retriever field trials and hunting tests. The Irish Water Spaniel was represented in the very first Westminster Kennel Club Show in 1877 and was the first sporting dog to obtain an AKC® obedience title. Irish Water Spaniels also excel in agility, rally, dock diving, freestyle, tracking, and flyball, and they serve as therapy and assistance dogs.

Official Standard for the Irish Water Spaniel

General Appearance: That of a smart, upstanding, strongly built moderate gun dog bred for all types of shooting, especially for water-fowling. Great intelligence is combined with rugged endurance and a bold, dashing eagerness of temperament.

Irish Water Spaniel

Distinguishing characteristics are a topknot of long, loose curls and a body covered with a dense, crisply curled liver colored coat contrasted by a smooth face and a smooth "rat tail."

Size, Proportion, Substance: Strongly built and well-boned, the Irish Water Spaniel is of medium length making it slightly rectangular in appearance. A well-balanced dog that should not appear leggy or coarse.

Size: Height: Dogs 22 to 24 inches (measured at the highest point of withers); Bitches: 21 to 23 inches. Weight: Dogs 55 to 68 pounds; Bitches: 45 to 58 pounds.

Head and Skull: The head is cleanly chiseled. The skull is large and high in dome with a prominent occiput and a gradual stop. The muzzle is long, deep and somewhat square in appearance with a strong underjaw. Lips are fine in texture, tight and dry. The nose is large and dark liver in color. The teeth are even with a scissor or level bite. Hair on the face is short and smooth except for a beard of long, loose curls growing at the back of the lower jaw which may continue up the side of the face as sideburns.

Topknot: A characteristic of the breed, the topknot consists of long, loose curls covering the skull and falling down over the top of the ears and occiput. The contrast between the smooth face and the topknot is evident in a well-defined peak between the eyes. The topknot, a breed characteristic, should not be trimmed in an exaggerated or excessive manner.

Eyes: Set almost flush, the eyes are comparatively small and almond shaped with tight eyelids. The color is a warm tone of medium to dark brown, dark amber but never yellow. The expression is keenly alert, intelligent, direct and quizzical.

Ears: Long, lobular, set low, hanging close to the head and abundantly covered with long loose curls of hair.

Neck, Topline, Body: *Neck*—The neck is long, arching, strong and muscular and is smoothly set into cleanly sloping shoulders. *Topline*—The rear is equal to or slightly higher than the front never descending or showing sag or roach. *Back*—Strong, broad and level. *Body*—Medium length. The ribs are carried well back and so well sprung behind the shoulders as to give a barrel shape. The chest is deep with a brisket extending to the elbows. The loin is short, wide, muscular, and deep so it does not give a tucked-up appearance.

Forequarters: The entire front gives the impression of strength without heaviness. The forechest should be moderate. Shoulders are sloping and moderately laid back, clean and powerful. The upper arms are approximately the length of the shoulder blades with clean elbows set close to the body. Forelegs are well boned, muscular and straight, set well under the withers.

Hindquarters: Sound hindquarters are of great importance to provide drive and power while swimming. They are as high as or slightly higher than the shoulders with powerful, muscular, well-developed thighs. The hips are wide. The croup is rounded and full with the tail set on low enough to give a rounded appearance. The stifles are moderately bent. Hocks are set low and moderately bent. Balance of front and rear angulation is important.

Feet: Large, round, somewhat spreading. Well clothed with hair. Pads are thick.

Tail: The "rat tail" is a striking characteristic of the breed and is strong, low set and carried level with the back and is not quite long enough to reach the point of the hock. The tail is thick at the root where it is covered for 2 to 3 inches with short curls which stop abruptly. From that point the tail is covered with smooth hair and the tail tapers to a fine point.

Coat: Proper coat is of vital importance to protect the dog while working. The coat on the face is short and smooth framed by the distinctive topknot and ears

of long, loose curls. The coat on the throat is smooth forming a V-shaped patch from the back of the lower jaw behind the beard to the breastbone. The remainder of the neck, body and base of the tail are covered with dense, tight, crisp curls. The remainder of the coat on the tail is short and smooth coated. Forelegs are covered down to the feet with curls or waves all around. The hind legs are also abundantly covered with curls or waves except that the hair is short and smooth on the front of the legs below the hocks. Feet are well clothed with hair. Dogs may be shown in natural coat or trimmed. However, no dog should be groomed or trimmed so excessively as to obscure the curl or texture of the coat.

Color: Rich liver to dark liver with a purplish tinge, sometimes called puce liver. No white hair or markings except for the graying of age.

Gait: Moves freely and soundly with balanced reach and drive. Should be true, precise and not slurring; may have a characteristic rolling motion accentuated by the barrel-shaped rib cage.

Temperament: Very alert, inquisitive and active. Stable in temperament with an endearing sense of humor. May be reserved with strangers but never aggressive or shy.

Faults: *The foregoing description is that of the ideal adult Irish Water Spaniel in hard working condition. Any deviation from the above-described dog must be considered to the extent of the deviation, keeping in mind the importance of various features toward the basic original purpose of the breed, which is that of a gun dog used for work in all types of shooting and particularly suited to water fowling in difficult marshy terrain.*

Approved July 14, 2009
Effective September 1, 2009

Meet the Labrador Retriever

Recognized by AKC® in 1917
Labrador Retriever Club (thelabradorclub.com), formed in 1931

Traits
- Loving
- Energetic
- Friendly

HISTORY

The Labrador Retriever did not originate in Labrador but on the island of Newfoundland. In all probability, the breed developed from a combination of European breeds brought to Newfoundland on numerous fishing ships. These ships' dogs, along with other dogs brought by English, Irish, and French colonists, combined in the melting pot that was colonial Newfoundland to produce the Labrador Retriever.

The shorthaired black dogs were known as Lesser Newfoundlands or St. John's Dogs until several were purchased by the Third Earl of Malmsbury from fishermen on vessels returning to England. Malmsbury wrote, "We always call mine Labrador dogs…," and he developed a breeding program to preserve their retrieving instinct and willingness to please.

The breed soon attracted the attention of sportsmen in the United States, and Labradors were imported back to this continent in the early part of the twentieth century. The first Labrador was registered by the American Kennel Club® in 1917, and the breed has since been utilized not only as a hunting dog but also as an assistance dog, substance-detection dog, search and rescue worker, and, its most important job, family companion. Because of his versatility and good nature, the Labrador has been the most popular AKC®-registered breed in the United States since 1992.

FORM AND FUNCTION

Although the Labrador is the master of many trades, his essence is that of a working retriever. For this reason, the muzzle is the same length as the back skull, enabling gentle handling of game; the neck is long enough to pick up game easily; the forechest is a prow shape to break water and ice; the body is keel-shaped for water stability; the feet are medium-sized and well webbed for strong propulsion in water; the two coats wrap the body as feathers and down wrap a duck; and the thick unique "otter" tail serves as a rudder. Finally, it is the retrieving instinct and intelligent, friendly, outgoing attitude that gives us the hallmark temperament of the breed.

AKC Official Guide to Sporting Dogs

All Labrador Retrievers in the United States originate from dogs imported from England and come in three coat colors—black, yellow, and chocolate. You may find breeders who concentrate on bloodlines for either field work or show competition, although many Labradors are able to do both. Dogs from field lines tend to be lighter built and more energetic. Consider your lifestyle and interests when selecting your future puppy.

LIVING WITH A LAB

Adding a Labrador Retriever to your family is a serious obligation. Labradors are energetic, devoted, intelligent, and enthusiastic companions who need to be included in family activities. They are willing learners, easily trained, and have sweet, loving dispositions. They are not suited for protection or guard duties.

To add a healthy, well-socialized Labrador to your family, seek a reputable breeder with an interest in helping you understand the breed and who uses the Orthopedic Foundation for Animals (OFA) and the American College of Veterinary Ophthalmologists (ACVO) to clear breeding stock. The Labrador's popularity has resulted in an increase in casual and unethical breeders whose concern is monetary. Be patient and do your research before making a commitment.

Labrador puppies are very mouth-oriented and can do serious damage to almost any surface. Adolescent puppies are strong and need consistent leadership from their owners, as well as obedience training and exercise. The Labrador's favorite activities are retrieving and swimming. The Labrador's short, dense coat requires little grooming beyond regular brushing; however, the coat does shed heavily twice a year. A Labrador is easy to feed. In fact, the breed is disposed to overeating. Owners need to monitor food intake and provide regular exercise. A simple check for proper weight is to be able to feel ribs, but never see them.

COMPETITION

Labrador Retrievers participate in an interesting variety of AKC® events, including conformation, obedience, tracking, agility, and rally. Performance events, which test what the dogs were bred to do, include retriever field trials, hunting tests, and the LRC's working certificate test.

Official Standard for the Labrador Retriever

General Appearance: The Labrador Retriever is a strongly built, medium-sized, short-coupled dog possessing a sound, athletic, well-balanced conformation that enables it to function as a retrieving gun dog; the substance and soundness to hunt waterfowl or upland game for long hours under difficult conditions; the character and quality to win in the show ring; and the temperament to be a family companion. Physical features and mental characteristics should denote a dog bred to perform as an efficient retriever of game with a stable temperament suitable for a variety of pursuits beyond the hunting environment.

The most distinguishing characteristics of the Labrador Retriever are its short, dense, weather resistant coat; an "otter" tail; a clean-cut head with broad back skull and moderate stop; powerful jaws; and its "kind," friendly eyes, expressing character, intelligence and good temperament.

Above all, a Labrador Retriever must be well balanced, enabling it to move in the show ring or work in the field with little or no effort. The typical Labrador possesses style and quality without over refinement, and substance without lumber or cloddiness. The Labrador is bred primarily as a working gun dog; structure and soundness are of great importance.

Size, Proportion, and Substance: *Size*—The height at the withers for a dog is 22½ to 24½ inches; for a bitch is 21½ to 23½ inches. Any variance greater than ½ inch above or below these heights is a disqualification. Approximate weight of dogs and bitches in working condition: dogs 65 to 80 pounds; bitches 55 to 70 pounds.

The minimum height ranges set forth in the paragraph above shall not apply to dogs or bitches under twelve months of age.

Proportion—Short-coupled; length from the point of the shoulder to the point of the rump is equal to or slightly longer than the distance from the withers to the ground. Distance from the elbow to the ground should be equal to one half of the height at the withers. The brisket should extend to the elbows, but not perceptibly deeper. The body must be of sufficient length to permit a straight, free and efficient stride; but the dog should never appear low and long or tall and leggy in outline. *Substance*—Substance and bone proportionate to the overall dog. Light, "weedy" individuals are definitely incorrect; equally objectionable are cloddy lumbering specimens. Labrador Retrievers shall be shown in working condition well-muscled and without excess fat.

Head: *Skull*—The skull should be wide; well developed but without exaggeration. The skull and foreface should be on parallel planes and of approximately equal length. There should be a moderate stop—the brow slightly pronounced so that the skull is not absolutely in a straight line with the nose. The brow ridges aid in defining the stop. The head should be clean-cut and free from fleshy cheeks; the bony structure of the skull chiseled beneath the eye with no prominence in the cheek. The skull may show some median line; the occipital bone is not conspicuous in mature dogs. Lips should not be squared off or pendulous, but fall away in a curve toward the throat. A wedge-shape head or a head long and narrow in muzzle and back skull is incorrect as are massive, cheeky heads. The jaws are powerful and free from snippiness—the muzzle neither long and narrow nor short and stubby. *Nose*—The nose should be wide and the nostrils well-developed. The nose should be black on black or yellow dogs, and brown on chocolates. Nose color fading to a lighter shade is not a fault. A thoroughly pink nose or one lacking in any pigment is a disqualification. *Teeth*—The teeth should be strong and regular with a scissors bite; the lower teeth just behind, but touching the inner side of the upper incisors. A level bite is acceptable, but not desirable. Undershot, overshot, or misaligned teeth are serious faults. Full dentition is preferred. Missing molars or pre-molars are serious faults. *Ears*—The ears should hang moderately close to the head, set rather far back, and somewhat low on the skull; slightly above eye level. Ears should not be large and heavy, but in proportion with the skull and reach to the inside of the eye when pulled forward. *Eyes*—Kind, friendly eyes imparting good temperament, intelligence and alertness are a hallmark of the breed. They should be of medium size, set well apart, and neither protruding nor deep set. Eye color should be brown in black and

yellow Labradors, and brown or hazel in chocolates. Black or yellow eyes give a harsh expression and are undesirable. Small eyes, set close together or round prominent eyes are not typical of the breed. Eye rims are black in black and yellow Labradors, and brown in chocolates. Eye rims without pigmentation is a disqualification.

Neck, Topline, Body: *Neck*—The neck should be of proper length to allow the dog to retrieve game easily. It should be muscular and free from throatiness. The neck should rise strongly from the shoulders with a moderate arch. A short, thick neck or a "ewe" neck is incorrect. *Topline*—The back is strong and the topline is level from the withers to the croup when standing or moving. However, the loin should show evidence of flexibility for athletic endeavor. *Body*—The Labrador should be short-coupled, with good spring of ribs tapering to a moderately wide chest. The Labrador should not be narrow chested; giving the appearance of hollowness between the front legs, nor should it have a wide spreading, bulldog-like front. Correct chest conformation will result in tapering between the front legs that allows unrestricted forelimb movement. Chest breadth that is either too wide or too narrow for efficient movement and stamina is incorrect. Slab-sided individuals are not typical of the breed; equally objectionable are rotund or barrel chested specimens. The underline is almost straight, with little or no tuck-up in mature animals. Loins should be short, wide and strong; extending to well developed, powerful hindquarters. When viewed from the side, the Labrador Retriever shows a well-developed, but not exaggerated forechest. *Tail*—The tail is a distinguishing feature of the breed. It should be very thick at the base, gradually tapering toward the tip, of medium length, and extending no longer than to the hock. The tail should be free from feathering and clothed thickly all around with the Labrador's short, dense coat, thus having that peculiar rounded appearance that has been described as the "otter" tail. The tail should follow the topline in repose or when in motion. It may be carried gaily, but should not curl over the back. Extremely short tails or long thin tails are serious faults. The tail completes the balance of the

AKC Official Guide to Sporting Dogs

Labrador Retriever

Labrador by giving it a flowing line from the top of the head to the tip of the tail. Docking or otherwise altering the length or natural carriage of the tail is a disqualification.

Forequarters: Forequarters should be muscular, well coordinated and balanced with the hindquarters. *Shoulders*—The shoulders are well laid-back, long and sloping, forming an angle with the upper arm of approximately 90 degrees that permits the dog to move his forelegs in an easy manner with strong forward reach. Ideally, the length of the shoulder blade should equal the length of the upper arm. Straight shoulder blades, short upper arms or heavily muscled or loaded shoulders, all restricting free movement, are incorrect. *Front legs*—When viewed from the front, the legs should be straight with good strong bone. Too much bone is as undesirable as too little bone, and short legged, heavy boned individuals are not typical of the breed. Viewed from the side, the elbows should be directly under the withers, and the front legs should be perpendicular to the ground and well under the body. The elbows should be close to the ribs without looseness.

Tied-in elbows or being "out at the elbows" interfere with free movement and are serious faults. Pasterns should be strong and short and should slope slightly from the perpendicular line of the leg. Feet are strong and compact, with well-arched toes and well-developed pads. Dewclaws may be removed. Splayed feet, hare feet, knuckling over, or feet turning in or out are serious faults.

Hindquarters: The Labrador's hindquarters are broad, muscular and well-developed from the hip to the hock with well-turned stifles and strong short hocks. Viewed from the rear, the hind legs are straight and parallel. Viewed from the side, the angulation of the rear legs is in balance with the front. The hind legs are strongly boned, muscled with moderate angulation at the stifle, and powerful, clearly defined thighs. The stifle is strong and there is no slippage of the patellae while in motion or when standing. The hock joints are strong, well let down and do not slip or hyper-extend while in motion or when standing. Angulation of both stifle and hock joint is such as to achieve the optimal balance of drive and traction.

When standing the rear toes are only slightly behind the point of the rump. Over-angulation produces a sloping topline not typical of the breed. Feet are strong and compact, with well-arched toes and well-developed pads. Cow-hocks, spread hocks, sickle hocks and over-angulation are serious structural defects and are to be faulted.

Coat: The coat is a distinctive feature of the Labrador Retriever. It should be short, straight and very dense, giving a fairly hard feeling to the hand. The Labrador should have a soft, weather-resistant undercoat that provides protection from water, cold and all types of ground cover. A slight wave down the back is permissible. Woolly coats, soft silky coats, and sparse slick coats are not typical of the breed, and should be severely penalized.

Color: The Labrador Retriever coat colors are black, yellow and chocolate. Any other color or a combination of colors is a disqualification. A small white spot on the chest is permissible, but not desirable. White hairs from aging or scarring are not to be misinterpreted as brindling. *Black*—Blacks are all black. A black with brindle markings or a black with tan markings is a disqualification. *Yellow*—Yellows may range in color from fox-red to light cream, with variations in shading on the ears, back, and underparts of the dog. *Chocolate*—Chocolates can vary in shade from light to dark chocolate. Chocolate with brindle or tan markings is a disqualification.

Movement: Movement of the Labrador Retriever should be free and effortless. When watching a dog move toward oneself, there should be no sign of elbows out. Rather, the elbows should be held neatly to the body with the legs not too close together. Moving straight forward without pacing or weaving, the legs should form straight lines, with all parts moving in the same plane. Upon viewing the dog from the rear, one should have the impression that the hind legs move as nearly as possible in a parallel line with the front legs. The hocks should do their full share of the work, flexing well, giving the appearance of power and strength. When viewed from the side, the shoulders should move freely and effortlessly, and the foreleg should reach forward close to the ground with extension. A short, choppy movement or high knee action indicates a straight shoulder; paddling indicates long, weak pasterns; and a short, stilted rear gait indicates a straight rear assembly; all are serious faults. Movement faults interfering with performance, including weaving; side-winding; crossing over; high knee action; paddling; and short, choppy movement, should be severely penalized.

Temperament: True Labrador Retriever temperament is as much a hallmark of the breed as the "otter" tail. The ideal disposition is one of a kindly, outgoing, tractable nature; eager to please and non-aggressive towards man or animal. The Labrador has much that appeals to people; his gentle ways, intelligence and adaptability make him an ideal dog. Aggressiveness towards humans or other animals or any evidence of shyness in an adult should be severely penalized.

Disqualifications: 1. *Any deviation from the height prescribed in the Standard.* 2. *A thoroughly pink nose or one lacking in any pigment.* 3. *Eye rims without pigment.* 4. *Docking or otherwise altering the length or natural carriage of the tail.* 5. *Any other color or a combination of colors other than black, yellow or chocolate as described in the Standard.*

Approved February 12, 1994
Effective March 31, 1994

Meet the Lagotto Romagnolo

Recognized by AKC® in 2015
Lagotto Romagnolo Club of America (lagottous.com), formed in 2007

Traits
- Affectionate
- Undemanding
- Energetic

HISTORY

The Lagotto Romagnolo dates back to Italy's pre-Roman Etruscan civilization and remained a common sight through medieval times. During the sixteenth century, the Lagotto was the inseparable companion, guardian, and retriever of the Vallarolo people, the inhabitants of the Valle San Giovanni in the Abruzzi region of Italy. The dogs accompanied the local gentry while they hunted the game-rich lagoons. Dredging over several decades reduced the immense marsh of Romagna; soon, the Vallaroli almost disappeared, and the Lagotto's role as water dog was not needed.

His sharp aptitude for searching, strong hunt drive, and limitless sense of smell gave the Lagotto another job—truffle hunter. This transition took place between 1840 and 1890. Within fifty years, nearly all the truffle dogs in Romagna and the surrounding regions were Lagottos. Truffle hunters nurtured lines that enhanced the breed's keen sense of smell and drive to work. Some crossbreeding may have occurred when the numbers of dogs dwindled.

During the 1970s, a group of Lagotto lovers led by Quintino Toschi, Professor Francesco Ballotta, Dr. Antonio Morsiani, and Lodovico Babini worked to save the Lagotto Romagnolo from extinction. Since the 1990s, numbers of Lagottos and registrations in Switzerland, Holland, Germany, France, Finland, Great Britain, Australia, and the United States have risen steadily. The breed became a fully recognized member of the AKC® Sporting Group on July 1, 2015.

FORM AND FUNCTION

The Lagotto is a water dog of small to medium size with a stocky trunk, a coat consisting of well-defined ring-shaped curls, and a thick undercoat. His general appearance is rustic, strong, and well proportioned. The expression is one of attentiveness, intelligence, and vivacity. The Lagotto works enthusiastically and efficiently, making the most of his inherent search-and-find skills and excellent sense of smell. He is an affectionate animal who forms a close bond with his owner and also makes a fine, easy-to-train companion. His character is that of the true country dog, with the gentle, attentive expression typical of all dogs of Italian descent. The Lagotto's coat comes in brown, roan, white, off-white, and orange. The ears are triangular but round on the ends, and faces are full of curly hair.

LIVING WITH A LAGOTTO

When selecting your puppy, always expect the breeder to health test all breeding stock regularly. Few health problems exist in the breed. The Lagotto Romagnolo is a very energetic dog who requires exercise to stay mentally and physically healthy. They are well suited to active families and love games like fetch or hide and seek. All Lagottos naturally love the water. They do require some coat care, but it is not as extensive as for many breeds. They have hair instead of fur and therefore are low shedding and sometimes acceptable for people with allergies. The hair needs to be trimmed on a regular basis.

COMPETITION

The Lagotto Romagnolo can compete in all companion events, including obedience, tracking, agility, and rally, as well as in conformation. With their beautiful movement and charming personalities, they are sure to be a show favorite.

Official Standard for the Lagotto Romagnolo

General Appearance: Small to medium-sized dog, well-proportioned, powerfully built, of rustic appearance, with a dense, curly coat of wooly texture. The dog should give the impression that he has the strength and endurance to work all day in difficult and challenging terrain.

Size, Substance, Proportions: *Size*—Height at the withers: Dogs 16½ to 19½ inches; Bitches 15½ to 18½ inches. Disqualification—Dog under 16½ or over 19½ inches; bitches under 15½ or over 18½ inches. Substance—Males 28 to 35 pounds. Females 24 to 31 pounds. *Important Proportions*—The Lagotto is a square dog, measured from the prosternum to the point of ischium and from the highest point of the shoulder to the ground. The length of the head is 40 percent of the height at the withers. The neck is slightly shorter than the length of the head. The length of the skull should be slightly more than half the length of the head. The legs are slightly more than half the height of the dog at the shoulder.

Head: Viewed from above and from the side, the *head* is a broad blunted wedge. The length of the skull, from stop to occiput, is the same as the width at the widest point of the zygomatic arch. The somewhat arched skull is slightly longer than half the length of the head (56 percent skull to 44 percent muzzle) with unpronounced occiput. Planes of the *skull* and *muzzle* diverge slightly—extreme divergence, parallel planes or dish faced appearance are serious faults. Nasal bone is straight. The stop is moderate, with a distinct furrow between the eyes. Frontal sinuses are well developed, giving good fill beneath the eye. Cheeks are flat. The wide robust underjaw defines the shape of the muzzle so that the lips form an upside-down semi-circle. The nose is large with wide open and mobile nostrils and a strongly pronounced median groove. It protrudes very slightly from the front edge of

AKC Official Guide to Sporting Dogs

the lips. The nose should be fully pigmented in shades from light to dark brown, varying with coat color. Anything else is a serious fault. Lips are rather tight and not thick. The strong lower jaw determines the profile of the muzzle. The flews are tight fitting and dry. Pigment of the lips varies with coat color from light to dark brown. Well- developed teeth meet, ideally, in a scissor or level *bite*. A reverse scissor bite is acceptable. Full dentition is preferred. Disqualification—Overshot or undershot bites (where the incisors do not touch those of the opposing jaw). The *eyes* are set somewhat frontal-obliquely, and fairly well apart. They are large, rounded, fill the sockets, and very slightly protruding. The color of the iris ranges from ochre to hazel to dark brown–no other colors are acceptable. Eyelids are close fitting. Eye rim color will vary with coat color from light to dark brown. Eyelashes are very well developed. The arch of the eyebrow is prominent. The *ears* are medium-sized in proportion to the head, triangular with rounded tips. The base of the ear is rather wide and is set just above the zygomatic arch. When alert, the top of the ear rises to widen the appearance of the skull, and the front edge of the ear is close to the cheek. When pulled loosely forward, the ear should cover about ¼ of the length of the muzzle. The Lagotto's expression should be intelligent, friendly and attentive.

Neck, Body, Topline: The *neck* is strong muscular, thick, and oval in shape. It is lean, well set off from the nape, and slightly arched. The length of neck is slightly less than the total length of the head. Neck should blend smoothly into shoulders. Muscles are extremely powerful. A correct neck is fundamental to function. The Lagotto *body* is square, compact and strong. The length of the dog, measured from the prosternum to the point of the ischium, should be the same as the height at the top of the scapulae, which are long and quite high-set, rising well above the level of the back. Chest is wide and well-developed, reaching down to the elbows, but not below them. The ribcage is slightly narrowed in front, widening from the sixth rib back, allowing elbows to move smoothly along the body. Ribs are well sprung (width of ribcage at the widest point is about 30 percent of the height of the dog). Underline is straight, with a slight tuck-up at the flank. The scapulae are set high, back straight, loin slightly arched, croup slightly sloping and tail follows the line of the croup. A line drawn from the top of the shoulder to the hip will be slightly sloping. A dog high in the rear or low in the withers is to be penalized. The Lagotto's back is straight and very muscular. The loin is short-coupled, very strong, and slightly arched. Its width is equal to or slightly exceeds the length, giving strength for digging. Croup is slightly sloped, quite long, broad, and muscular. It forms an angle of approximately 25 to 30 degrees from the horizontal. Flat or steep croups are to be severely penalized. The *tail* is set on following the line of the croup. At rest, it is carried scimitar-like, and no higher than the back. When excited, the tail is decidedly raised, and carried in a loose arc above the level of the back. Tip of tail should not be carried further forward than the pelvis. The tail should never be curled or carried straight up. The tail tapers from base to end, and should reach to just above the hock. Ringtails or tails carried over the back are serious faults.

Forequarters: The shoulder blades are long (30 percent at the height of the withers), well laid back (yet not too close at tips), muscular, and strong. They are closely attached to the chest, but move freely. The angle formed between the shoulder

blade and the upper arm should be approximately 115 degrees. The elbow will fall on a vertical line lowered from the back of the scapula to the ground. The upper arm is as long as the shoulder blade, of light bone structure, muscular, and tucked firmly against the brisket. Legs are straight. The forearm is long, with strong, compact, oval bone. The carpus is fine, robust and mobile, and in complete alignment with the forearm. Pasterns are also in perfect alignment with forearm, and of slightly finer bone. They are moderate in length and slightly sloping. Forefeet are webbed, rounded, and compact, with well-arched, tight toes. Pads have particularly hard soles. Nails are curved and range in color from white to extremely dark brown.

Hindquarters: Angulation of the hindquarter is slightly less than the angle of the forequarter (approximately 110 degrees). Legs are powerful and parallel when seen from the rear. The upper thigh is slightly longer than the shoulder (35 percent of height at withers). It is quite broad, convex, and with well-defined muscles. The second thigh is slightly longer than the upper thigh, well boned and strong. The hindquarters must be perfectly parallel to the spine. The angle of the stifle should be more open than the angle at the hip, (approximately 130 degrees). The hock joint is well let down, wide, clean and strong. Pasterns are thin, cylindrical, and perpendicular to the ground when the dog is standing freely. A vertical line from the point of buttocks to the ground will fall slightly in front of the toes. Hind feet are slightly oval, compact, and webbed. The toes of the back feet are not quite as arched as those of the forefeet; thus, the nails may be straighter.

Skin, Coat: The skin of the Lagotto is thin, firm and close-fitting all over the body, without wrinkles. Pigmentation of the skin and pads harmonizes with the color of the coat, ranging from dark pink to dark brown. Depigmentation anywhere on the body is a serious fault. Coat is extremely important in this breed. Hair should be of wooly texture, semi-rough on the surface. Topcoat should be quite thick, and undercoat visible. The combination of the two repel water. A correct coat is never luxurious or shiny. The body is covered with tight ring-shaped curls, not frizz. Skull and cheeks are covered with thick hair, and the looser curls of the head form abundant eyebrows, whiskers, and a rather bristly beard. The coat covering the tail is both curly and somewhat bristly. The Lagotto must not be corded. Disqualification—smooth or straight coat. The correct trim must always be unpretentious, and contribute to the natural, rustic look typical of the breed. In a curled state the body coat must be trimmed to no more than 1½ inches in depth (not brushed/combed out), and it should be uniform with the silhouette of the dog. Only on the head can the coat be longer than 1½ inches, but should never cover the eyes (should be penalized). The edges of the ears should be trimmed to the leather; the surface of the ear flap should show looser curls, but remain wavy. The area around the genitals and anus may be clipped short. Hair must be of sufficient length that curls and texture can be assessed. Corded dogs or excessively groomed dogs (sculpted or blown out) should be so severely penalized as to be eliminated from competition.

Color: Lagotti can be off-white solid color, white with brown or orange patches, brown roan, orange roan, brown, orange, or sable (in different shades), with or without white. Some dogs have extremities darker than their body color. Tan markings (in different shades) allowed. The colors have a tendency to fade, sometimes to such an extent that the brown areas can appear as silvery/gray roan. All the above colors are equally desirable, including the faded or diluted colors. Disqualification—Black or gray coat or patches; black pigmentation.

Gait/Movement: Lagotti should exhibit an energetic, lively, balanced trot, with moderate reach and drive. Back should remain firm and strong with no tendency to roll. At a trot, the rear foot covers but does not pass the footprint of the front foot. Movement from the front is parallel at a walk or slow trot, never wider than the dog's shoulder, and tends toward a center line as speed increases. Rear legs are also parallel at a slow gait, converging at increased speed, with hocks staying in a straight line between hip and foot. As the dog increases speed, the neck moves slightly lower and forward. The Lagotto should move with distinction and nobility of bearing. He should not be exhibited in an elongated trot—it is atypical and incorrect for the breed.

Behavior, Temperament: The Lagotto is tractable, adaptable, keen, affectionate, and extremely attached to its owner. He is both highly intelligent and easily trained. He is an excellent companion and a very good watchdog. A natural gift for searching and a very good nose have made the breed very efficient in finding truffles. The former hunting instinct has been modified by genetic selection to avoid distraction by game. This breed should never be aggressive or overly shy.

Faults: Any departure from the foregoing points should be considered a fault and the seriousness with which the fault should be regarded should be in exact proportion to its degree and to the degree that it will affect the dog's ability to perform its traditional work, as well as the health and welfare of the dog.

Disqualifications:

Size—Dogs under 16½ inches or over 19½ inches. Bitches under 15½ inches or over 18½ inches.
Bite—Overshot or pronounced undershot bite (incisors of the upper jaw and lower jaw do not touch).
Coat—Smooth or straight.
Color—Black or gray coat or patches; black pigmentation.

Approved January 14, 2020
Effective March 31, 2020

Meet the Nederlandse Kooikerhondje

Recognized by AKC® in 2018
Nederlandse Kooikerhondje Club of the United States of America (nkcusa.org); formed in 1997

Traits
- Cheerful
- Quick
- Devoted

HISTORY

Lively, agile, and highly intelligent, the Nederlandse Kooikerhondje (pronounced *NAY-der-lond-suh COY-ker-hond-juh*) has a long history as both a hard worker and a devoted companion. The breed was developed centuries ago in the Netherlands, with a job of assisting duck trappers who captured the waterfowl using a system of ditches and canals enclosed with willow screens; it was found that the curious birds could be lured into the trap by the energetic little dog waving his trademark white plume of a tail while trotting along the banks. The dogs were also skilled at catching and killing vermin along the canals, yet they were loving and sweet-natured at home; the breed was prized in the region. They were a favorite among the nobility and are featured in many Dutch paintings from the seventeenth through the nineteenth centuries.

By the early twentieth century, however, the use of the traditional duck-trapping system had declined in the Netherlands, and, as World War II ravaged Europe, the breed's numbers dwindled. The Kooikerhondje would likely have disappeared forever were it not for the efforts of the Baroness van Hardenbroek van Ammerstol. In the 1940s, the baroness, a devoted dog fancier, enlisted the help of a traveling salesman to search the Dutch countryside for remnants of the breed, giving the man a description and a sample of the coat. Eventually a female dog named Tommie was found in the Friesland region in the north, and the baroness was able to raise two litters of puppies from Tommie. Afterward, she continued to rebuild the breed for several decades. Though still somewhat rare today, the breed now boasts healthy numbers and has a dedicated following around the world.

Nederlandse Kooikerhondje

FORM AND FUNCTION

The Kooiker (*COY-ker*), as his fans often call him, is always orange-red and white in color. His appealing face is framed by well-feathered ears often featuring the desirable long, black hair-tips known in the breed as "earrings." The breed's small-to-medium size makes the Kooiker a great travel companion, and they are physically very agile and athletic. They are also extremely responsive mentally, being "tuned in" to their humans to an almost uncanny degree, and readily picking up on human emotions. They are very smart and eager to please and can learn tricks and commands with amazing speed. Kooikers are also highly sensitive; this must always be kept in mind, and harsh punishments or training methods must never be used.

LIVING WITH A NEDERLANDSE KOOIKERHONDJE

With this sensitive breed, it is vital for the young Kooiker to be gently exposed to many different kinds of people, settings, and experiences throughout puppyhood and up to the age of two years to help ensure that the dog matures into an adaptable companion who is at ease in many situations. Care should be taken so that this socialization is always positive and never scary or intimidating for the young dog.

Kooikers love being physically and mentally active. They enjoy frequent outings with their owners, as well as games and canine sports that allow them to expend energy in a safe setting. They have cheerful personalities, and they bond to their owners with great devotion, although they can be reserved and wary with strangers. Their many fine qualities notwithstanding, the breed is not for every household; with sensitivity to loud noises and sudden movements, a Kooiker might not be a good match for a setting where, for example, he is around boisterous young children for most of the day. That said, the breed can make wonderful family dogs and loving companions to children they are raised with. Many Kooikers do not tolerate being around unfamiliar or rough-playing dogs. Visiting dog parks is not recommended for the breed.

There are a few health conditions the breed may be prone to, but dedicated breeders are diligent about doing health testing and making responsible breeding decisions, thus Kooikers are generally quite healthy overall. The breed's handsome, silky coat needs no more than weekly brushing and minimal bathing.

COMPETITION

This very smart, athletic, and versatile breed excels in a wide range of canine sports and activities. The Kooiker's speed has him often earning high rankings in fast-paced events such as agility and Fast CAT®; with his high intelligence and trainability, he's a star in obedience and rally too. Kooikers also shine in Barn Hunt, dock diving, Trick Dog™, and other challenging competitions. Additionally, the breed gains notice in the conformation show ring.

Official Standard for the Nederlandse Kooikerhondje

General Appearance: The Nederlandse Kooikerhondje is a harmoniously built orange-red parti-colored small sporting dog of almost square body proportions. He moves with his head held high; in action, the well-feathered waving tail is carried level with, or above the topline. The ears may have black hair at the tips, the so-called earrings. The dog is presented with a natural, untrimmed coat. Visible scissoring or grooming, except for neatening the feet, is to be severely penalized.

Size Proportion, Substance: Size—Ideal height at the withers: Males 16 inches, Females 15 inches. Disqualification—1½ inches under the ideal height after 1 year of age or 1½ inches above the ideal height at any age. Proportion—Skull and muzzle are of about equal length. The length of the body from the point of the shoulder (at the scapula/humerus) to the point of the buttocks should be slightly longer than the height at the withers. Length of forelegs from ground to elbow should be equal to depth of body from elbow to withers. Substance—strong bone, but not heavy.

Head: The head is of moderate length, fitting in with the general appearance, clean-cut, with flowing lines. Eyes—Almond-shaped, dark brown with a friendly, alert expression. Ears—Medium size, set above eye level but always lower than the top of the skull. The ears are carried close to the cheeks without a fold. Ear leather should easily reach the inner corner of the eye. Well feathered. Black hair tips ("earrings") are highly desirable. Skull—Sufficiently broad, moderately rounded. Stop—Seen in profile clearly visible but not too deep. Muzzle—Should be a blunt wedge seen from above or in profile, not too deep, nor tapering too much. Well filled under the eye, creating a smooth transition from muzzle to skull. Planes (Muzzle & Skull)—Straight muzzle, almost parallel planes. Nose—Black and well developed. Lips—Preferably well pigmented, close fitting and not pendulous. Bite—Scissors bite. Complete dentition preferable.

Nederlandse Kooikerhondje

Level bite acceptable, but less desirable.

Neck, Topline, Body: Neck—Medium length to balance body, clean-cut and strongly muscled. Topline—Smooth level line from the withers to hipbones with a slightly rounded croup. Chest—Reaching to the elbows with moderate spring of ribs. Underline—Slight tuck-up towards the loin. Back—Strong and straight, rather short. Loin—Short and broad, strongly muscled. Tail—Set on so as to follow the topline of the body. Well-feathered with a white plume. The last vertebra should reach the hock joint. When gaiting, carried level with the topline, with an upward curve or almost straight up. Not curling with a ring or circling over the back. When standing, the tail may be held downward.

Forequarters: Shoulders—Shoulder moderately angled in order to create a flowing line from neck to back. Upper Arm—Moderately angled to match layback of shoulder blade, which is of equal length. Forechest—Prosternum—Point of forechest should be slightly protruding beyond the point of the shoulder. Elbow—Close to the body. Legs—Straight and parallel, strong bone of sufficient density and length. Pasterns—Strong and slightly oblique. Forefeet—Small, slightly oval, compact, toes pointing forward.

Hindquarters: Angulation—Moderately angulated, to match forequarters. Seen from the rear, straight and parallel. Legs—Strong bone. Upper Thigh—well muscled. Second Thigh—length equal to upper thigh. Hock Joint—well let down. Hind Feet—Small, oval, compact, toes pointing forward.

Coat: Hair—Of medium length, close lying. May be slightly wavy or straight, but never curly or open. Soft, but with enough texture to be weather resistant. Functional undercoat. Front legs should have moderate feathering reaching to the pastern joints. Hind legs should have fairly long feathered breeches. No feathering below the hock joints. The coat on the head, the front part of the legs and the feet should be short. Sufficiently feathered on the underside of the tail. Longer hair on throat and forechest. Earrings (long feathered black hair tips) are highly desirable.

Color: Distinct patches of clear orange-red on pure white are ideal. A few small spots on the legs or muzzle are acceptable. Chest, belly, and the majority of the legs and tail should be white.

Orange red color should predominate on the head and torso and may be present as a mantle or blanket, but is less desirable than distinct patches. Some black hair intermingling with the orange-red color and a slight form of ticking are acceptable, but less desirable. A black tail ring where the color changes from orange-red to white on the tail is permitted.

Coloring on the head: A clearly visible white blaze running down to the nose. There should be coloring on the cheeks, ideally ending at the corners of the mouth, and around the eyes. A blaze that is too narrow or too wide or only partly colored cheeks is less desirable. Color should be a consideration only when all else between two dogs is equal. Disqualification—Color that is black and white or tri-color.

Gait: Should be flowing and light-footed, with moderate reach and drive. Limbs parallel. Temperament: Lively and agile, self-confident and with sufficient perseverance and stamina. Good natured and alert, however not noisy. The breed is faithful, easygoing and friendly to his owners and can be a bit reserved with strangers. When not luring ducks into elaborate man-made traps, the dog is expected to find and kill vermin, and to alert his family to strangers on the property. Hence he needs to be keen, swift and tough. He is a true sporting dog, being attentive and energetic and having a zest for working and with a cheerful character.

Faults: Any departure from the foregoing points should be considered a fault and the seriousness with which the fault should be regarded should be in exact proportion to its degree and the functional health and welfare of the dog and on its ability to perform its traditional work. Ears too small. Ears half-erect, "flying ears." Tail that is too curled. Hackney gait. Curly or silky hair. Open coat. Color that is heavily interspersed with black hairs in the orange-red patches. Too much ticking.

Severe Faults: Anxious behavior. Distinctly low on legs, out of proportion. Blue or yellow eye(s). Undershot or overshot bite. Tail too short, vertebrae not reaching hock-joint. White color on ears, partly or completely. White hair around eyes, one or both.

Disqualifications: *1½ inches under the ideal height after 1 year of age or 1½ inches above the ideal height at any age. Color that is black and white or tri-color.*

Approved February 10, 2017
Effective April 1, 2017

Meet the Nova Scotia Duck Tolling Retriever

Recognized by AKC® in 2003
Nova Scotia Duck Tolling Retriever Club (USA) (nsdtrc-usa.org), formed in 1984

HISTORY

Nova Scotia Duck Tolling Retrievers (Tollers) originated in the province of Nova Scotia, Canada, probably in the early to mid-1800s. There is no authentic record of the breed's origins. Current thinking is that the basic stock was the red decoy dog brought to Canada by the early Acadian (French) settlers. They were subsequently crossed with a setter type, spaniel type, retriever type, and farm collie. Originally called Yarmouth Tollers or Little River Duck Dogs, taking their name from the area of Nova Scotia where they were found, they were first registered with the Canadian Kennel Club in 1945 and given the name Nova Scotia Duck Tolling Retriever.

To *toll* means to lure. The hunter is hidden, usually in natural cover, while ducks or geese are rafting out on the water. The hunter throws a ball or stick along the shoreline, and the dog retrieves it. The ducks are attracted to the Toller's animated retrieving and come in close to investigate. The hunter stands, flares the ducks into flying, and shoots. The Toller then retrieves the ducks.

Tollers were first seen in the United States in the 1930s at sportsmen's shows. Some were imported in the 1960s, but it wasn't until the late 1970s and early 1980s that serious breeders began to take an interest. A national club was formed in 1984 and gained AKC® recognition on July 1, 2003.

FORM AND FUNCTION

The Toller was bred to retrieve from the cold inland lakes and ocean off Nova Scotia. His double coat protects him from the cold, and his thick neck cape

protects the blood vessels leading to the brain. The Toller is a medium-sized dog, large enough to handle a duck or smaller goose, but small enough to live in a small home. He is an active dog as befits his tolling heritage.

LIVING WITH A TOLLER

People interested in owning a Toller should choose a breeder who will work with them in selecting the best puppy for their family, lifestyle, and interests. Most Toller breeders will, after careful evaluation of their litter, choose the pup who best fits a prospective home. Since Tollers have a variety of white markings, breeders will pay little attention to this aspect when selecting a pup.

Tollers are happiest in an active household. They require calm consistency and clear directions from their owners and work best with praise. They are an intelligent, thinking, and sometimes manipulative breed that requires an owner who appreciates the challenge of training.

Besides good-quality food and regular veterinary exams, Tollers need exercise, including daily walks, runs several times a week, and plenty of retrieving. Tollers should have a job to keep their brains engaged, whether that is bringing in the paper, retrieving the family hunter's ducks, or participating in one of the AKC®'s many sports. Toller puppies are very active and should attend puppy socialization and basic obedience classes. Tollers require weekly brushing, trimming of excess hair from their feet and ears, and regular teeth brushing.

COMPETITION

Tollers participate in AKC® hunting tests, retriever field trials, conformation, agility, obedience, rally, tracking, and flyball. Tollers make empathetic therapy and service dogs and are successful as search and rescue/avalanche dogs.

Official Standard for the Nova Scotia Duck Tolling Retriever

General Appearance: The Nova Scotia Duck Tolling Retriever (Toller) was developed in the early nineteenth century to toll, lure, and retrieve waterfowl. The playful action of the Toller retrieving a stick or ball along the shoreline arouses the curiosity of the ducks offshore. They are lured within gunshot range, and the dog is sent out to retrieve the dead or wounded birds.

This medium sized, powerful, compact, balanced dog is the smallest of the retrievers. The Toller's attitude and bearing suggest strength with a high degree of agility. He is alert, determined, and quick, with a keen desire to work and please.

Many Tollers have a slightly sad or worried expression when they are not working. The moment the slightest indication is given that retrieving is required, they set themselves for springy action with an expression of intense concentration and excitement. The heavily feathered tail is held high in constant motion while working.

The Nova Scotia Duck Tolling Retriever Club (USA) feels strongly that all Tollers should have these innate abilities and encourages all Tollers to prove them by passing an approved Nova Scotia Duck Tolling Retriever Club (USA) field test.

Size, Proportion, and Substance—*Size:* Height at the withers—Males, 18 to 21 inches. The ideal is 19 inches. Females, 17 to 20 inches. The ideal is 18 inches. *Bone* is medium. *Weight* is in proportion to height and bone of the dog. The dog's length should be slightly longer than height, in a ratio of 10 to 9, but should not give the impression of a long back.

Head—*Skull:* The head is clean-cut and slightly wedge shaped. The broad skull is only slightly rounded, giving the appearance of being flat when the ears are alert. The occiput is not prominent. The cheeks are flat. The length of the skull from the occiput to the stop is slightly longer than the length of the muzzle from the stop to the tip of the nose. The head must be in proportion to body size. *Expression:* The expression is alert, friendly, and intelligent. Many Tollers have a slightly sad expression until they go to work, when their aspect changes to intense concentration and desire. *Eyes:* The eyes are set well apart, slightly oblique and almond in shape. Eye color blends with the coat or is darker. Eye rims must be self-colored or black, matching the nose and lips. *Faults:* Large round eyes. Eye rims and/or eyes not of prescribed color. *Ears:* The high set ears are triangular in shape with rounded tips, set well back on the skull, framing the face, with the base held slightly erect. Ear length should reach approximately to the inside corners of the eyes. Ears should be carried in a drop fashion. Ears are short-coated, and well feathered only on the back of the fold. **Stop:** The stop is moderate. *Muzzle:* The muzzle tapers in a clean line from stop to nose, with the lower jaw not overly prominent. The jaws are strong enough to carry a sizeable bird, and softness in the mouth is essential. The underline of the muzzle is strong and clean. *Fault:* Dish face. *Nose:* The nose is fairly broad with the nostrils well open, tapering at the tip. The color should blend with that of the coat, or be black. *Fault:* Bright pink nose. *Disqualification: Butterfly nose. Lips and flews:* Lips fit fairly tightly, forming a gentle curve in profile, with no heaviness in the flews. *Bite:* The correct bite is tight scissors. Full dentition is required. *Disqualifications: Undershot bite. Wry mouth. Overshot by more than 1/8 inch.*

Neck, Backline, Body—*Neck:* The neck is strongly muscled and well set on, of medium length, with no indication of throatiness. *Backline:* Level. *Faults:* Roached or sway back. *Body:* The body is deep in chest, with good spring of rib, the brisket reaching to the elbow. Ribs are neither barrel shaped nor flat. The back is strong, short and straight. The loins are strong and muscular, with moderate tuck-up. *Fault:* Slack loins. *Tail:* The tail follows the natural very slight slope of the croup, is broad at the base, and is luxuriant and well feathered, with the last vertebra reaching at least to the hock. The tail may be carried below the level of the back except when the dog is alert, when it is held high in a curve, though never touching the body. *Faults:* tail too short, kinked, or curled over touching the back. Tail carried below the level of the back when the dog is gaiting.

Forequarters: The shoulder should be muscular, strong, and well angulated, with the blade roughly equal in length to the upper arm. The elbows should work close to the body, cleanly and evenly. When seen from the front, the foreleg's appearance is that of parallel columns. The pasterns are strong and slightly sloping. *Fault:* Down in the pasterns. **Feet:** The feet are strongly webbed, slightly oval, medium in size, and tight, with well-arched toes and thick pads. Front dewclaws may be removed. *Faults:* Splayed or paper feet.

Hindquarters: The hindquarters are muscular, broad, and square in appearance. The **croup** is very slightly sloped. The rear and front angulation should be in balance. The upper and lower thighs are very muscular and equal in length. The stifles are well bent. The hocks are well let down, turning neither in nor out. Rear dewclaws must not be present. *Disqualification: Rear dewclaws.*

Coat: The Toller was bred to retrieve from icy waters and must have a water-repellent double coat of medium length and softness, and a soft dense undercoat. The coat may have a slight wave on the back, but is otherwise straight. Some winter coats may form a long loose curl at the throat. Featherings are soft and moderate in length. The hair on the muzzle is short and fine. Seasonal shedding is to be expected. Overcoated specimens are not appropriate for a working dog and should be faulted. While neatening of the feet, ears, and hocks for the show ring is permitted, the Toller should always appear natural, never barbered. Whiskers must be present. *Faults:* Coat longer than medium length. Open coat.

Color: Color is any shade of red, ranging from a golden red through dark coppery red, with lighter featherings on the underside of the tail, pantaloons, and body. Even the lighter shades of golden red are deeply pigmented and rich in color. *Disqualifications: Brown coat, black areas in coat, or buff. Buff is bleached, faded, or silvery. Buff may also appear as faded brown with or without silver tips.*
Markings: The Toller has usually at least one of the following white markings: tip of tail, feet (not extending above the pasterns), chest and blaze. A dog of otherwise high quality is not to be penalized for lack of white. *Disqualifications: White on the shoulders, around the ears, back of neck, or across the flanks.*

Gait: The Toller combines an impression of power with a springy gait, showing good reach in front and a strong driving rear. Feet should turn neither in nor out, and legs travel in a straight line. In its natural gait at increased speeds, the dog's feet tend to converge towards a center line, with the backline remaining level.

Temperament: The Toller is highly intelligent, alert, outgoing, and ready for action, though not to the point of nervousness or hyperactivity. He is affectionate and loving with family members and is good with children, showing patience. Some individuals may display reserved behavior in new situations, but this is not to be confused with shyness. Shyness in adult classes should be penalized. The Toller's strong retrieving desire coupled with his love of water, endurance and intense birdiness, is essential for his role as a tolling retriever.

Disqualifications: *Butterfly nose. Undershot bite, wry mouth, overshot by more than $1/8$ inch. Rear dewclaws. Brown coat, black areas in coat, or buff. Buff is bleached, faded or silvery. Buff may also appear as faded brown, with or without silver tips. White on the shoulders, around the ears, back of the neck, or across the flanks.*

Approved June 11, 2001
Effective September 1, 2001

Meet the Pointer

Recognized by AKC® in 1884
American Pointer Club (americanpointerclub.org), formed in 1938

Traits
- Active
- Hardworking
- Loyal

HISTORY

Pointers have existed for centuries throughout the European continent, arriving in England around 1650. They originally served as locaters of hares for Greyhounds to pursue or game birds hiding in cover to be held on point until netted. As firearms evolved for wing-shooting, some sportsmen in England crossed the Pointer with other breeds (mainly Foxhounds for endurance, Bloodhounds for increased scenting ability, and Greyhounds for speed, etc.) to gain various advantages for this faster paced sport. These crosses produced a downside as unintended hound traits manifested themselves in this already excellent air-scenting breed. By the early 1800s, these characteristics were judiciously being eliminated, and this grand gun dog has changed little since then.

Pointers were brought to America prior to the Civil War and steadily gained popularity. By the 1870s, importations from the British Isles increased substantially, and Pointers were among the first eight breeds to be registered in the United States. They were recognized by the American Kennel Club® when it was formed in 1884, and their type holds true to the standard today when seen competing at modern AKC® dog shows, field, and other performance events.

The Pointer has always been bred for type as well as field ability, but by the 1930s, a divergence was apparent in America. Today, the AKC®-registered "show" Pointer continues to embody the physical standard with game-seeking ability, while the more numerous "field" Pointer, registered with the Field Dog Stud Book, concentrates on field ability.

FORM AND FUNCTION

This handsome sporting dog fills the eye with its short, smooth coat, clean limbs, and musculature that disguise nothing. His head is unique among the gun dogs, with chiseled features that are both beautiful and functional. He carries it high, with nostrils flaring to catch the scent of game on the wind instead of on the ground. At that magical moment, all forward motion ceases and the Pointer stands frozen as he awaits the hunter's approach to flush the quarry. As with his forebears and contemporaries in England, the tail is a near-level extension off his back and is anatomically incapable of being raised high.

LIVING WITH A POINTER

Pointers are active! Should a Pointer puppy be your heart's desire, know that this bright-eyed, winsome package will grow into an exuberant 45- to 75-pound athlete with a need for physical and mental exercise. A reputable breeder will provide access to the pup's parents (photos if not on-site), their health history (and clearances), and advice.

Ideally, a Pointer's owner is one who, besides providing care, shelter, and companionship, gives the gift of time each day for one-on-one exercise and play. Providing a securely fenced yard for your Pointer to stretch his legs to burn off some of that renowned "hunt all day" endurance is most beneficial and will make him even more livable inside the home. If you plan to hunt with him, his nose won't be ruined by indoor aromas, nor will his desire to please in the field be lessened by finding his place beside you and your family on the sofa (or bed).

Pointers are easy to maintain: a soft brush or hand-brushing keeps year-round shedding to a fair minimum, and baths are not necessary more than a few times a year, unless circumstances warrant it. Nail trimming, gentle ear cleaning, and tooth brushing complete this "wash 'n wear" breed's grooming needs.

Generally healthy, Pointers enjoy a lifespan of between ten to fourteen years.

COMPETITION

Pointers are versatile! AKC®-registered Pointers are eligible for conformation, pointing-dog field trials, hunting tests, obedience, tracking, agility, and rally events. Many Pointers have multiple titles before and after their name, indicating their ability to perfect their inherent talents and happily learn new ones. Pointers have also been known to excel at service and therapy work, as well as in search and rescue.

Official Standard for the Pointer

General Appearance: The Pointer is bred primarily for sport afield; he should unmistakably look and act the part. The ideal specimen gives the immediate impression of compact power and agile grace; the head noble, proudly carried; the expression intelligent and alert; the muscular body bespeaking both staying power and dash. Here is an animal whose every movement shows him to be a

AKC Official Guide to Sporting Dogs

wide-awake, hard-driving hunting dog possessing stamina, courage, and the desire to go. And in his expression are the loyalty and devotion of a true friend of man.

Temperament: The Pointer's even temperament and alert good sense make him a congenial companion both in the field and in the home. He should be dignified and should never show timidity toward man or dog.

Head: The skull of medium width, approximately as wide as the length of the muzzle, resulting in an impression of length rather than width. Slight furrow between the eyes, cheeks cleanly chiseled. There should be a pronounced stop. From this point forward the muzzle is of good length, with the nasal bone so formed that the nose is slightly higher at the tip than the muzzle at the stop. Parallel planes of the skull and muzzle are equally acceptable. The muzzle should be deep without pendulous flews. Jaws ending square and level, should bite evenly or as scissors. Nostrils well developed and wide open.

Ears—Set on at eye level. When hanging naturally, they should reach just below the lower jaw, close to the head, with little or no folding. They should be somewhat pointed at the tip—never round—and soft and thin in leather. *Eyes*—Of ample size, rounded and intense. The eye color should be dark in contrast with the color of the markings, the darker the better.

Neck: Long, dry, muscular, and slightly arched, springing cleanly from the shoulders.

Shoulders: Long, thin, and sloping. The top of blades close together.

Front: Elbows well let down, directly under the withers and truly parallel so as to work just clear of the body. Forelegs straight and with oval bone. Knee joint never to knuckle over. Pasterns of moderate length, perceptibly finer in bone than the leg, and slightly slanting. Chest, deep rather than wide, must not hinder free action of forelegs. The breastbone bold, without being unduly prominent. The ribs well sprung, descending as low as the elbow-point.

Back: Strong and solid with only a slight rise from croup to top of shoulders. Loin of moderate length, powerful and slightly arched. Croup falling only slightly to base of tail. Tuck-up should be apparent, but not exaggerated.

AKC Official Guide to Sporting Dogs

Pointer

Tail: Heavier at the root, tapering to a fine point. Length no greater than to hock. A tail longer than this or docked must be penalized. Carried without curl, and not more than 20 degrees above the line of the back; never carried between the legs.

Hindquarters: Muscular and powerful with great propelling leverage. Thighs long and well developed. Stifles well bent. The hocks clean; the legs straight as viewed from behind. Decided angulation is the mark of power and endurance.

Feet: Oval, with long, closely set, arched toes, well-padded, and deep. Catfoot is a fault. Dewclaws on the forelegs may be removed.

Coat: Short, dense, smooth with a sheen.

Color: Liver, lemon, black, orange; either in combination with white or solid-colored. A good Pointer cannot be a bad color. In the darker colors, the nose should be black or brown; in the lighter shades it may be lighter or flesh-colored.

Gait: Smooth, frictionless, with a powerful hindquarters' drive. The head should be carried high, the nostrils wide, the tail moving from side to side rhythmically with the pace, giving the impression of a well-balanced, strongly built hunting dog capable of top speed combined with great stamina. Hackney gait must be faulted.

Balance and Size: Balance and overall symmetry are more important in the Pointer than size. A smooth, balanced dog is to be more desired than a dog with strongly contrasting good points and faults. Hound or terrier characteristics are most undesirable. Because a sporting dog must have both endurance and power, great variations in size are undesirable, the desirable height and weight being within the following limits:

Dogs:
Height—25 to 28 inches
Weight—55 to 75 pounds

Bitches:
Height—23 to 26 inches
Weight—44 to 65 pounds

Approved November 11, 1975

Meet the Spinone Italiano

Recognized by AKC® in 2000
Spinone Club of America (spinoneclubofamerica.com), formed in 1987

Traits
- Sociable
- Patient
- Affectionate

HISTORY

The Spinone Italiano originated in the Piedmont region of Italy. Although the exact origin is uncertain, it is believed that today's Spinone descended from an ancient hunting breed, and its ancestors trace back to approximately 500 BC. In the early parts of the nineteenth century, there were several groups of dogs with Spinone characteristics existing in various regions of Italy, in both the white and orange and the brown roan colors but with differing coat textures. The first breed standard was written in 1897. During World War II, there were few Spinoni available for breeding, necessitating some outcrosses to such breeds as the German Wirehaired Pointer, the Wirehaired Pointing Griffon, and the Bracco Italiano. Fortunately, a small group of enthusiasts selectively bred the post-war dogs and retained the Spinone's conformation and working ability. The first known pair of Spinoni in the United States was imported in 1931. The breed was accepted into the AKC® Miscellaneous Class in March 1955 (although a Spinone Italiano was entered in the Miscellaneous Class at Westminster in 1932 and 1933), where it remained until it entered the Sporting Group on September 27, 2000.

FORM AND FUNCTION

The Spinone Italiano has been called the canine equivalent of an all-terrain vehicle. The terrain and cover in which these dogs originally worked required a rugged and sure-footed dog, capable of hunting in marshes and swamps, as well as in the steep and rocky mountainous regions of the heart of Italy. He is an endurance trotter who must navigate very steep inclines and crevices and enter heavy, thorny cover. The minimal break in the topline at the eleventh vertebrae allows the dog to twist and turn in ways other breeds cannot. The wide placement of the scapulae allows the dog to be flexible and loose. The robust and strongly built frame of the dog ensures that he is capable of handling the challenges of cover and terrain. The long head and muzzle and divergent head planes (the muzzle pointing down) allow the dog to smell his game while keeping his head up to navigate the mountains.

LIVING WITH A SPINONE

When selecting a Spinone puppy, be sure to do plenty of research to find a reputable, responsible breeder who registers puppies with AKC®, is active in shows and/or trials, and does all the recommended health testing, in addition to asking you plenty of questions and answering all of yours.

Consider your lifestyle when choosing a puppy. Do you want a dog who is very active and will demand a lot of your attention? Be aware that if a Spinone does not get enough attention and exercise, destructive habits can develop. It will be your job to provide enough activity for your puppy throughout his lifetime. Within every litter, there are pups with higher and lower activity levels, and finding the best fit will enrich both your life and the pup's.

Do you want a show dog? A home companion? A hunting partner? These are all things to discuss with the breeder in order to find the best fit for you. Temperament is also an important consideration, along with health. A healthy Spinone puppy should be sturdy and strong with clean ears, bright, clear eyes, and a happy attitude.

COMPETITION

Spinoni are eligible to participate in numerous AKC® events, including conformation shows, rally, obedience and agility trials, tracking, pointing-breed field trials, and pointing and retriever hunting tests. All of these activities can be extremely rewarding ways to work with your Spinone.

Official Standard for the Spinone Italiano

General Appearance: The Spinone has a distinctive profile and soft, almost-human expression. The breed is constructed for endurance. Muscular, vigorous and with powerful bone, the Spinone has a robust build that makes him resistant to fatigue and able to work on almost any terrain; big feet and a two-piece topline give the dog stability on rough ground. The Spinone covers ground efficiently, combining a purposeful, easy trot with an intermittent gallop. A harsh, single coat and thick skin enable the Spinone to negotiate underbrush and endure cold water that would punish any dog not so naturally armored. This versatile pointer is a proficient swimmer and an excellent retriever by nature. The Spinone is patient, methodical and cooperative in the field, and has a gentle demeanor.

Size, Proportion, Substance: The height at the withers is 23½ to 27½ inches for males and 22½ to 25½ inches for females. Weight: In direct proportion to size and structure of a dog in working condition. *Proportion*: His build tends to fit into a square. The length of the body, measured from the point of the shoulder to the point of the buttocks, is equal to or slightly greater than the height at the withers. *Substance*: The Spinone is a solidly built dog with powerful bone.

Head: Long, with muzzle length equal to that of the backskull. The length of the *head* is equal to 4/10 of the height at the withers; its width measured at the zygomatic arch is less than half of its total length. The profile of the Spinone is unusual. The occipital protuberance is well developed, and the upper longitudinal profiles of the skull and muzzle are divergent, downfaced, i.e., if extended, the top line of the muzzle emerges in front of or tangential to the occipital protuberance. A dish-faced muzzle is to be faulted so severely as to eliminate from further competition. The *skull* is oval, with sides gently sloping from the sagittal suture in a curve to the zygomatic arch. Cheeks are lean. The medial-frontal furrow is very pronounced. *Muzzle*—Stop is barely perceptible. Bridge of the muzzle is straight or slightly Roman. Square when viewed from the front. The width of the nasal bridge measured at its midpoint is a third of its length. The upper lips are rather soft and are rounded in front. The lower profile of the muzzle is created by the lower line of

the upper lip. *Eyes*—A soft sweet expression is of paramount importance to the breed. It shall denote intelligence and gentleness. Ochre (a soft golden brown) in color, darker eyes with darker colored dogs, lighter eyes with lighter colored dogs. The eyes are large, almost round, well opened, and set well apart on the frontal plane. The lid fits the eye closely. The eye is neither protruding nor deep set. Eye rim is clearly visible and will vary in color from flesh colored to brown depending on the color of the dog. Loose eyelids must be faulted.

Disqualification:
—Walleye (an eye with a whitish iris; a blue eye, fisheye, pearl eye). Nose—Large, bulbous and spongy in appearance with a rounded upper edge. Nostrils are large and well opened. In profile, the nose protrudes past the forward line of the lips. Pigment is a rosy flesh color in white-and-orange dogs, brown in brown-and-white or brown-roan dogs; in solid-white dogs, it can range from flesh colored to brown. Disqualification—Any pigment other than described or total depigmentation of the nose. Teeth—Jaw is powerful; at mid-length, the sides of the mandible are very lightly curved. Teeth are positioned in a scissors or level *bite*.

—Overshot or undershot bite. *Ears*—Almost triangular in shape with a slightly rounded tip, they are set on a level with the eye; long, but not more than 2 inches below the line of the throat; pendulous, carried close to the head and with little erectile power. The leather is fine, covered with short, thick hair mixed with longer sparser hair, which becomes thicker along the edges. The forward edge is adherent to the cheek, not curled, but turned back on itself.

Neck, Topline, Body: *Neck*—Strong, thick, and muscular, clearly defined from the nape, blending into the shoulders in a harmonious line. The length of the neck shall not be less than two-thirds of the length of the head. The throat is moderate in skin with a double dewlap. Chest—Broad, deep, well-muscled and well rounded; extending at least to the elbow. The ribs are well sprung. The distance from ground to the elbow is equal to ½ the height at the withers. Back—The *topline* consists of two segments. The first slopes slightly downward in a nearly straight line from the withers to the eleventh thoracic vertebra. The second rises gradually and continues into a solid and slightly convex loin without rising above the withers. The underline is solid. It is almost horizontal in the sternal region, then ascends only slightly towards the belly; there is minimal tuck-up. Croup—Wide, well-muscled, long. The hipbones fall away from the spinal column at an angle of about 30 to 35 degrees, producing a lightly rounded, well filled-out croup. *Tail*—Follows the line of the croup, thick, with no fringes. The tail is carried horizontally or down, flicking from side to side while trotting. The tail is customarily docked to a length of 6 to 10 inches. The structure and carriage of an undocked tail are consistent with those of a docked tail.

Forequarters: Shoulders—The shoulders are strong, well-muscled, long and well laid back; they are capable of moving freely and form an angle with the upper arm of approximately 105 degrees. The tops of the shoulder blades are not close together. The upper arm is of equal length to the shoulder blade. Angulation of shoulder is in balance with angulation in the rear. Forelegs: The forelegs are straight when viewed from the front, with strong, oval bone, well-developed muscles and well-defined tendons; elbows are set under the withers and close to the body. Pasterns are long, lean and flexible, following the vertical line of the forearm. In profile, they are slightly slanted. Feet—Front feet are large, compact, rounded, with well-arched toes which are close together, covered with short, dense hair, including between the toes. Pads are lean and hard with strong nails curving toward the ground, well pigmented, but never black. Dewclaws may be present.

Hindquarters: Thighs are strong and well-muscled, stifles show good functional angulation, lower thigh to be well developed and muscled with good breadth. The distance from the point of the hock to the ground is about one-third of the height at the withers, and the rear pastern is strong, lean and perpendicular to the ground. Feet—The rear foot is slightly more oval than the forefoot, with the same characteristics. Dewclaws may be present on the inner side of the rear pastern.

Skin: The skin must be very thick, closely fitting the body. The skin is thinner on the head, throat, groin, under the legs and in the folds of the elbows, where it is soft to the touch.

Pigmentation is dependent upon the color or markings of the coat. Disqualification: Any black pigmentation.

Coat: A Spinone must have a correct, harsh, single coat to be of correct type. There is no undercoat. The ideal coat length is 1½ to 2½ inches on the body. The hair is shorter on the head, ears, and along the top of the muzzle and front sides of legs and feet. The hair on the back sides of the legs forms a rough brush, but there are never any fringes. The eyes and lips are framed by long, stiff hair forming eyebrows, mustache and beard. The coat is coarse, dense and rather flat. The Spinone is exhibited in a natural state, in accordance with his function as a field dog.

Color: The accepted colors are: Solid white, white and orange; orange roan with or without orange markings; white with brown markings, and brown roan with or without brown markings. The most desired color of brown is a chestnut, "monk's habit" brown, however, other shades of brown are acceptable. Disqualification—Any black in the coat, tri-color in any combination, tan points or any color other than accepted colors.

Gait: He has a free, relaxed trot, geared for endurance. This trot, with intermittent gallop, allows the Spinone to cover maximum ground with the least amount of effort. Profile of the topline is kept as the dog trots.

Temperament: Sociable, docile, affectionate and patient.

Faults: Any departure from the foregoing points constitutes a fault which when judging must be penalized according to its seriousness and extent. Any characteristic that interferes with the accomplishment of the function of the Spinone shall be considered a serious fault.

Disqualifications:

Walleye (an eye with a whitish iris; a blue eye, fisheye, pearl eye.) Any pigment other than described or total depigmentation of the nose. Overshot or undershot bite. Any black pigmentation.

Any black in the coat; tri-color markings in any combination, tan points or any color other than accepted colors.

Approved August 14, 2018
Effective January 1, 2019

Meet the Sussex Spaniel

Recognized by AKC® in 1884
Sussex Spaniel Club of America (sussexspaniels.org), formed in 1981

Traits
- Even-Tempered
- Affectionate
- Friendly

HISTORY

The Sussex Spaniel got his name from Sussex, England, where the breed originated. Written records first mention the Sussex in 1803. A. E. Fuller, Esq., was active in breeding them and is mentioned frequently from the 1850s on. Mr. Fuller and Phineas Bullock did notable work in the breed and were surely the most influential breeders of the time. However, Joy Freer (Fourclovers Kennels) actually saved the breed from extinction during World War II. All Sussex today go back to the dogs she saved. Breeders today can and do proudly state that the Sussex of today have not changed in appearance since the Sussex of the 1850s.

The AKC® lists the Sussex as one of the first original nine breeds that it recognized, but the breed never became popular because there were faster, flashier gun dogs. Then, in the 1970s, American breeders revived these golden liver spaniels with the serious, frowning faces. In 2009, many people got their first glimpse of this rare breed when Ch. Clussexx Three D Grinchy Glee, now known worldwide as "Stump," made history by becoming the first Sussex Spaniel and the oldest dog of any breed, at age ten, to win Best in Show at the prestigious Westminster Kennel Club dog show.

FORM AND FUNCTION

The Sussex was originally bred as a hunting dog, ideal for going through heavy brush, hedgerows, and undergrowth. His long, low body with heavy bone was developed for this goal.

LIVING WITH A SUSSEX

A buyer doesn't really "select" a Sussex puppy. There are so few available that it would be a rare thing for a puppy buyer to be allowed to come to a breeder's home and choose from a litter of puppies. An informed puppy buyer is one who contacts a breeder or breeders and gets on a waiting list for a puppy. Sussex are rarer than pandas! In a good year, there will be sixty puppies born in the United States

and perhaps an equal number in other countries. Sometimes this can mean a waiting period of a year or more, but a Sussex baby is well worth waiting for.

A Sussex owner should be sure to socialize a puppy. Sussex puppies need to be introduced to whatever they will encounter in their lives—children, other dogs, cats, and more. Since Sussex are bird dogs, owners should keep pet birds well out of reach no matter how much those pleading Sussex eyes ask to play with one! Sussex need a regular amount of exercise, but this should never be forced, especially with puppies, because they need to be allowed to grow without excess stress on bones. While agility courses are now seen at dog parks and doggy day cares, it is a bad idea to allow a Sussex puppy to do any jumping before he is at least a year old.

Stairs are also a problem—Sussex puppies learn to go up pretty quickly, but coming down they tend to step on those low hanging ears and go tumbling. Until a Sussex is about six months old, the motto is "climb up and carry down."

A Sussex needs positive training. Obedience classes are wonderful, but an owner (or trainer) should never get rough with a Sussex. Sussex remember both good and bad things, and if they are hurt, they will never forget or truly forgive. Praise, practice, and perseverance are key.

Grooming is easy! Wash the dog, trim the toenails, and trim the hair from the bottom of the feet once a month. Comb and brush the dog a couple of times a week. The main problem is ears: they hang down in food, water, and anything on the ground. Keeping them brushed out and combed will keep them from matting.

COMPETITION

The Sussex Spaniel is a very versatile dog. Besides being a great pet and conformation show dog, they can do well in obedience, rally, and agility. Sussex also compete in spaniel field trials, tracking, and hunting tests, and they can be wonderful therapy dogs. Some Sussex are active in search and rescue work.

Official Standard for the Sussex Spaniel

General Appearance: The Sussex Spaniel was among the first ten breeds to be recognized and admitted to the *Stud Book* when the American Kennel Club® was formed in 1884, but it has existed as a distinct breed for much longer. As its name implies, it derives its origin from the county of Sussex, England, and it was used there since the eighteenth century as a field dog. During the late 1800s the reputation of the Sussex Spaniel as an excellent hunting companion was well known among the estates surrounding Sussex County. Its short legs, massive build, long body, and habit of giving tongue when on scent made the breed ideally suited to penetrating the dense undergrowth and flushing game within range of the gun. Strength, maneuverability, and desire were essential for this purpose. Although it has never gained great popularity in numbers, the Sussex Spaniel continues today essentially unchanged in character and general appearance from those nineteenth-century sporting dogs.

The Sussex Spaniel presents a long and low, rectangular and rather massive appearance coupled with free movements and nice tail action. The breed has a somber and serious expression. The rich golden liver color is unique to the breed.

Size, Proportion, Substance: *Size*—The height of the Sussex Spaniel as measured at the withers ranges from 13 to 15 inches. Any deviation from these measurements is a minor fault. The weight of the Sussex Spaniel ranges between 35 and 45 pounds. *Proportion*—The Sussex Spaniel presents a rectangular outline as the breed is longer in body than it is tall. *Substance*—The Sussex Spaniel is muscular and rather massive.

Head: Correct head and expression are important features of the breed. *Eyes*—The eyes are hazel in color, fairly large, soft and languishing, but do not show the haw overmuch. *Expression*—The Sussex Spaniel has a somber and serious appearance, and its fairly heavy brows produce a frowning expression. *Ears*—The ears are thick, fairly large, and lobe-shaped and are set moderately low, slightly above the outside corner of the eye. *Skull and muzzle*—The skull is moderately long and also wide with an indentation in the middle and with a full stop. The brows are fairly heavy, the occiput is full but not pointed, the whole giving an appearance of heaviness without dullness. The muzzle should be approximately 3 inches long, broad, and square in profile. The skull as measured from the stop to the occiput is longer than the muzzle. The nostrils are well-developed and liver colored. The lips are somewhat pendulous. *Bite*—A scissors bite is preferred. Any deviation from a scissors bite is a minor fault.

Neck, Topline, Body: *Neck*—The neck is rather short, strong, and slightly arched, but does not carry

the head much above the level of the back. There should not be much throatiness about the skin. *Topline and body*—The whole body is characterized as low and long with a level topline. The chest is round, especially behind the shoulders, and is deep and wide which gives a good girth. The back and loin are long and very muscular both in width and depth. For this development, the back ribs must be deep. *Tail*—The tail is docked from 5 to 7 inches and set low. When gaiting the Sussex Spaniel exhibits nice tail action, but does not carry the tail above the level of the back.

Forequarters: The shoulders are well laid back and muscular. The upper arm should correspond in length and angle of return to the shoulder blade so that the legs are set well under the dog. The forelegs should be very short, strong, and heavily boned. They may show a slight bow. Both straight and slightly bowed constructions are proper and correct. The pasterns are very short and heavily boned. The feet are large and round with short hair between the toes.

Hindquarters: The hindquarters are full and well-rounded, strong, and heavily boned. They should be parallel with each other and also set wide apart—about as wide as the dog at the shoulders. The hind legs are short from the hock to the ground, heavily boned, and should seem neither shorter than the forelegs nor much bent at the hocks. The hindquarters must correspond in angulation to the forequarters. The hocks should turn neither in nor out. The rear feet are like the front feet.

Coat: The body coat is abundant, flat or slightly waved, with no tendency to curl. The legs are moderately well-feathered, but clean below the hocks. The ears are furnished with soft, wavy hair. The neck has a well-marked frill in the coat. The tail is thickly covered with moderately long feather. No trimming is acceptable except to shape foot feather, or to remove feather between the pads or between

the hock and the feet. The feather between the toes must be left in sufficient length to cover the nails.

Color: Rich golden liver is the only acceptable color and is a certain sign of the purity of the breed. Dark liver or puce is a major fault. White on the chest is a minor fault. White on any other part of the body is a major fault.

Gait: The round, deep and wide chest of the Sussex Spaniel coupled with its short legs and long body produce a rolling gait. While its movement is deliberate, the Sussex Spaniel is in no sense clumsy. Gait is powerful and true with perfect coordination between the front and hind legs. The front legs do not paddle, wave, or overlap. The head is held low when gaiting. The breed should be shown on a loose lead so that its natural gait is evident.

Temperament: Despite its somber and serious expression, the breed is friendly and has a cheerful and tractable disposition.

Faults: The standard ranks features of the breed into three categories. The most important features of the breed are color and general appearance. The features of secondary importance are the head, ears, back and back ribs, legs, and feet. The features of lesser importance are the eyes, nose, neck, chest and shoulders, tail, and coat. Faults also fall into three categories. Major faults are color that is too light or too dark, white on any part of the body other than the chest, and a curled coat. Serious faults are a narrow head, weak muzzle, the presence of a topknot, and a general appearance that is sour and crouching. Minor faults are light eyes, white on chest, the deviation from proper height ranges, lightness of bone, shortness of body or a body that is flat-sided, and a bite other than scissors. There are no disqualifications in the Sussex Spaniel standard.

Approved April 7, 1992
Effective May 27, 1992

Meet the Vizsla

Recognized by AKC® in 1960
Vizsla Club of America (vcaweb.org), formed in 1953

Traits
- Athletic
- Intelligent
- Affectionate

HISTORY

A thousand years ago, the Vizsla hunted with Magyar nomads before settling into the region that is now Hungary. Primitive stone etchings show a Magyar tribal hunter with his falcon and his Vizsla. Centuries later, the Vizsla became the favored hunting and family dog of Hungarian aristocrats. In modern times, the Vizsla was almost wiped out as a breed by the World Wars before being imported to the United States in the 1950s. Since then, the Vizsla has thrived and developed into a versatile dog successful in many venues while maintaining his place as a premier gun dog and a lively, affectionate family member.

FORM AND FUNCTION

The Vizsla was built to cover fields with proficiency and grace. He is a medium-sized shorthaired sporting dog of rust-gold color that conveys elegance and readiness. In structure, the Vizsla appears balanced in height and length, with moderate angulation and substance. On the go, the Vizsla covers ground effortlessly with smooth movement and strong reach and drive. In the field, the Vizsla is a swift and careful hunter, with a superb nose and the best traits of a pointer and retriever. At home, the Vizsla exhibits a demeanor that is gentle, sweet, and sensitive.

LIVING WITH A VIZSLA

The Vizsla will thrive as an active member of the family. This breed is a great choice for someone wanting an athletic and active dog who will become a significant part of his or her life. Similarly, the Vizsla is a poor choice for someone wanting a dog who is expected to be content with two meals a day, a soft bed, and a walk around the block. Vizslas require physical and mental exercise on a daily basis. This redheaded child will push your lifestyle in his direction so much so that you will wonder how you ever lived without such a dog. A superb athlete and supreme snuggler, the Vizsla is a physically active and an emotionally attentive dog who needs to be outside with you and inside with you. The Vizsla is an intelligent and sensitive breed that aims to please. He takes to positive training with ease, and heavy-handed training should be avoided.

The Vizsla is a shorthaired dog who requires little or no grooming. The coat is easily cleaned and generally odor-free. However, contrary to common belief, the Vizsla does shed small red hairs. A Vizsla owner should be willing to commit to daily walks, hikes, hugs, and kisses mixed with positive training and socialization. Given proper exercise, training, and interaction, the Vizsla will be an amazing companion.

COMPETITION

The modern Vizsla has developed into a truly versatile dog. The Vizsla can participate successfully in multiple AKC® venues including conformation, obedience, agility, tracking, and therapy, while maintaining keen hunting instincts to excel in AKC® pointing-breed hunting tests and field-trial competitions. The breed's adaptability has extended it into roles working for the Transportation Security Administration, search and rescue groups, and assistance-dog programs.

Official Standard for the Vizsla

General Appearance: That of a medium-sized, short-coated hunting dog of distinguished appearance and bearing. Robust but rather lightly built, the coat is an attractive shaded golden rust. Originating in Hungary, the Vizsla was bred to work in field, forest and water. Agile and energetic, this is a versatile dog of power, drive and endurance in the field yet a tractable and affectionate companion in the home. It is strongly emphasized that field conditioned coats as well as brawny or sinewy muscular condition and honorable scars indicating a working and hunting dog are never to be penalized in this dog. The requisite instincts and abilities to maintain a "dual dog" are always to be fostered and appreciated, never deprecated.

Head: Lean and muscular. *Skull* moderately wide between the ears with a median line down the forehead. Stop between skull and foreface is moderate. Foreface or *muzzle* is of equal length or slightly shorter than skull when viewed in profile, should taper gradually from stop to tip of nose. Muzzle square and deep. It should not turn up as in a "dish" face nor should it turn down. Whiskers serve a functional purpose; their removal is permitted but not preferred. Nostrils slightly open. Nose self-colored. Any other color is faulty. *A partially or completely black nose is a disqualification.* Freckles due to aging or sun exposure are not to be faulted. *Ears*, thin, silky and proportionately long, with rounded-leather ends, set fairly low and hanging close to cheeks. *Jaws* are strong with well developed white teeth meeting in a scissors bite. *Eyes* medium in size and depth of setting, their surrounding tissue covering the whites. Color of the iris should blend with the color of the coat. Yellow or any other color is faulty. Prominent pop eyes are faulty. Lower eyelids should neither turn in nor out since both conditions allow seeds and dust to irritate the eye. *Lips* cover the jaws completely but are neither loose nor pendulous.

Neck and Body: *Neck* strong, smooth and muscular, moderately long, arched and devoid of dewlap, broadening nicely into shoulders which are moderately laid back. This is mandatory to maintain balance with the moderately angulated hindquarters. *Body* is strong and well proportioned. Withers high. While the Vizsla may appear square,

when measured from point of breastbone to point of buttocks and from the highest point over the shoulder blades to the ground, the Vizsla is slightly longer than tall. A proper proportion of leg length to body length is essential to the desired overall balance of the Vizsla. The Vizsla should not appear long and low or tall and leggy. Backline firm with a slight rise over a short and well muscled loin. The croup is gently rounded to the set on of the tail and is not steep, sunken or flat. When moving at a trot, a properly built Vizsla maintains a steady, level backline. *Chest* moderately broad and deep reaching down to the elbows. Ribs well-sprung and carried well back; underline exhibiting a slight tuck-up beneath the loin. *Tail* set just below the level of the croup, thicker at the root and docked one-third off. Ideally, it should reach to the back of the stifle joint and when moving it should be carried at or near the horizontal, not vertically or curled over the back, nor between the legs. A docked tail is preferred.

Forequarters: *Shoulder* blades proportionately long and wide sloping moderately back and fairly close at the top. Upper arm is about equal in length to the shoulder blade in order to allow for good extension. *Forelegs* straight and muscular with elbows close. Feet cat-like, round and compact with toes close. Nails brown and short. Pads thick and tough. The removal of dewclaws, if any, on front and rear feet, is strongly recommended, in order to avoid injury when running in the field.

Hindquarters: *Hind legs* have well developed thighs with moderately angulated stifles and hocks in balance with the moderately laid back shoulders. They must be straight as viewed from behind. Too much angulation at the hocks is as faulty as too little. The hocks are let down and parallel to each other.

Coat: Short, smooth, dense and close-lying, without woolly undercoat. *A distinctly long coat is a disqualification.*

Color: Golden rust in varying shades. Lighter shadings over the sides of the neck and shoulders giving the appearance of a "saddle" are common. Solid dark mahogany and pale yellow are faulty. White on the forechest, preferably as small as possible, and white on the toes are permissible. *Solid white extending above the toes or white anywhere else on the dog except the forechest is a disqualification.* When viewing the dog from the front, white markings on the forechest must be confined to an area from the top of the sternum to a point between the elbows when the dog is standing naturally. *White extending on the shoulders or neck is a disqualification.* White due to aging or scarring must not be faulted. The Vizsla is self-colored, with the color of the eyes, eye-rims, lips, nose, toenails and pads of feet blending with the color of the coat.

Gait: Far reaching, light footed, graceful and smooth. When moving at a fast trot, a properly built dog single tracks.

Size: The ideal male is 22 to 24 inches at the highest point over the shoulder blades. The ideal female is 21 to 23 inches. Because the Vizsla is meant to be a medium-sized hunter, any dog measuring more than 1½ inches over or under these limits must be disqualified.

Temperament: A natural hunter endowed with a good nose and above-average ability to take training. Lively, gentle-mannered, demonstrably affectionate and sensitive though fearless with a well developed protective instinct. Shyness, timidity or nervousness should be penalized.

The foregoing describes the ideal Vizsla. Any deviation from this ideal must be penalized to the extent of the deviation. Deviations that impact performance and function should be considered more serious than those that affect only appearance.

Disqualifications: *Partially or completely black nose. Solid white extending above the toes or white anywhere else on the dog except the forechest. White extending on the shoulders or neck. A distinctly long coat. Any male over 25½ inches or under 20½ inches and any female over 24½ inches or under 19½ inches at the highest point over the shoulder blades.*

Approved January 13, 2009
Effective April 1, 2009

Meet the Weimaraner

Recognized by AKC® in 1943
Weimaraner Club of America (weimaranerclubofamerica.org), formed in 1942

Traits
- People-Centric
- Fearless
- Energetic

HISTORY

The story of the Weimaraner begins in the dense, game-rich forests of central Germany. For centuries, this forested terrain was the exclusive hunting ground of the nobility. The Weimar region was famous for its cultural heritage and fostering the finer things in life. Included was the development of a unique breed of dog who would be a gentleman's hunting partner. Several breeds were used to create the Weimaraner, and its distinct type emerged around the turn of the nineteenth century. Originally, this all-purpose hunting dog was used on boar, bear, and deer, but, as big-game populations began to decline, the Weimaraner made the transition to smaller mammals and birds. Ownership was strictly limited to the ruling class, and specimens of the breed were closely held and greatly prized.

Although the breed characteristics were developed in the early nineteenth century, it was not until 1929 that the first Weimaraners reached US shores. It took more than a decade of Herculean efforts by American sportsman Howard Knight to be granted permission from the German Weimaraner Club to bring the first reproductively viable specimens to this country.

World War II gave Continental breeders impetus for getting quality dogs out of Europe and into the United States. In the 1950s, the Weimaraner became the "dog *de jour*" and was proclaimed the new wonder dog. Outlandish claims of super hunting prowess, uncanny intelligence, and trainability overpopularized the Weimaraner. As time passed, reality reasserted itself, and today the Weimaraner holds its rightful place as a versatile hunting breed, an excellent companion, and dog-sport competitor.

FORM AND FUNCTION

As hunting dogs, the Weimaraner is large, with a long level back, deep chest, and strong legs. Webbed feet allow the Weimaraner to swim with ease. Weimaraners are strong animals with stamina and a desire to work and play for long stretches of time.

A note on color: The breed is known as the "Gray Ghost," but they come in several shades from mouse-gray to silver-gray. Their amber, gray, or blue-gray eyes give them a unique expression.

LIVING WITH A WEIMARANER

If you decide to select the Weimaraner as the breed for you, remember that one of his core traits is that he is people-centric. Weims were developed to be kept in the house with the family and not relegated to a kennel. This strong inherent trait can lead to extreme separation anxiety. Puppies should be crate-trained and carefully taught that there will be times when the people of the household will not be in close proximity.

Being a big, active, intelligent hunting breed, the Weimaraner is not for owners who are frail of body or spirit. *Weimaraners need exercise!* These three little words cannot be overstressed. There must be an outlet for all their energy, and they prefer exercise they can do with you. They are delighted to join you in physical activities, revel in long runs in the field, and consider swimming on a hot summer day a treat beyond description. A fenced yard is strongly recommended.

Grooming a Weimaraner is simple, since the basics of doing nails and teeth make up the majority of the work. The short, sleek coats wash out and dry quickly, making baths a minor chore. The frequency of baths depends on where the dogs get to run. Being hunters, when they get to wander the fields, they will try to disguise their own scent by rolling in stinky things. They proudly and persistently put on "perfume" that only a creature with a perverse sense of smell would appreciate.

The Weimaraner's high energy and intelligence make training a must. A well-trained Weimaraner is a delight to live with, but an untrained one is akin to a canine demolition derby. Puppies should be started in classes at an early age. Training needs to be consistent and applied gently but firmly to channel their high energy and abilities. With knowledgeable training, even tiny puppies can learn basic obedience commands, point birds, and retrieve to hand. Once they learn something (whether it is a good thing or a bad thing), it's in their heads forever.

COMPETITION

Although Weimaraners were originally developed solely as hunting companions, they are remarkable in their versatility and excel in other AKC® events

beyond field work, which they thoroughly enjoy. They are excellent obedience, rally, and agility competitors. It's said that to enter a tracking event with a Weimaraner is "cheating" because the breed's scenting abilities are so keen and its persistence in pursuing a track so unerring.

Official Standard for the Weimaraner

General Appearance: A medium-sized gray dog, with fine aristocratic features. He should present a picture of grace, speed, stamina, alertness and balance. Above all, the dog's conformation must indicate the ability to work with great speed and endurance in the field.

Height: Height at the withers: dogs, 25 to 27 inches; bitches, 23 to 25 inches. One inch over or under the specified height of each sex is allowable but should be penalized. Dogs measuring less than 24 inches or more than 28 inches and bitches measuring less than 22 inches or more than 26 inches shall be disqualified.

Head: Moderately long and aristocratic, with moderate stop and slight median line extending back over the forehead. Rather prominent occipital bone and trumpets well set back, beginning at the back of the eye sockets. Measurement from tip of nose to stop equals that from stop to occipital bone. The flews should be straight, delicate at the nostrils. Skin drawn tightly. Neck clean-cut and moderately long. Expression kind, keen and intelligent. *Ears*—Long and lobular, slightly folded and set high. The ear when drawn snugly alongside the jaw should end approximately 2 inches from the point of the nose. *Eyes*—In shades of light amber, gray or blue-gray, set well enough apart to indicate good disposition and intelligence. When dilated under excitement the eyes may appear almost black. *Teeth*—Well set, strong and even; well-developed and proportionate to jaw with correct scissors bite, the upper teeth protruding slightly over the lower teeth but not more than $\frac{1}{16}$ of an inch. Complete dentition is greatly to be desired. *Nose*—Gray. *Lips and Gums*—Pinkish flesh shades.

Body: The back should be moderate in length, set in a straight line, strong, and should slope slightly from the withers. The chest should be well developed

AKC Official Guide to Sporting Dogs

and deep with shoulders well laid back. Ribs well sprung and long. Abdomen firmly held; moderately tucked-up flank. The brisket should extend to the elbow.

Coat and Color: Short, smooth and sleek, solid color, in shades of mouse-gray to silver-gray, usually blending to lighter shades on the head and ears. A small white marking on the chest is permitted, but should be penalized on any other portion of the body. White spots resulting from injury should not be penalized. A distinctly long coat is a disqualification. A distinctly blue or black coat is a disqualification.

Forelegs: Straight and strong, with the measurement from the elbow to the ground approximately equaling the distance from the elbow to the top of the withers.

Hindquarters: Well-angulated stifles and straight hocks. Musculation well developed.

Feet: Firm and compact, webbed, toes well arched, pads closed and thick, nails short and gray or amber in color. ***Dewclaws***—Should be removed.

Tail: Docked. At maturity it should measure approximately 6 inches with a tendency to be light rather than heavy and should be carried in a manner expressing confidence and sound temperament. A non-docked tail shall be penalized.

Gait: The gait should be effortless and should indicate smooth coordination. When seen from the rear, the hind feet should be parallel to the front feet. When viewed from the side, the topline should remain strong and level.

Temperament: The temperament should be friendly, fearless, alert and obedient.

Faults: *Minor faults*—Tail too short or too long. Pink nose. *Major faults*—Doggy bitches. Bitchy dogs. Improper muscular condition. Badly affected teeth. More than four teeth missing. Back too long or too short. Faulty coat. Neck too short, thick or throaty. Low-set tail. Elbows in or out. Feet east and west. Poor gait. Poor feet. Cow hocks. Faulty backs, either roached or sway. Badly overshot, or undershot bite. Snipy muzzle. Short ears. *Very serious faults*—White, other than a spot on the chest. Eyes other than gray, blue-gray or light amber. Black mottled mouth. Non-docked tail. Dogs exhibiting strong fear, shyness or extreme nervousness.

Disqualifications: *Deviation in height of more than 1 inch from standard either way. A distinctly long coat. A distinctly blue or black coat.*

Approved December 14, 1971

Meet the Welsh Springer Spaniel

Recognized by AKC® in 1906
Welsh Springer Spaniel Club of America (wssca.com), formed in 1961

Traits
- Upbeat
- Loyal
- Family Companion

HISTORY

The Welsh Springer Spaniel is a breed of ancient origin, dating at least as far back as the 1500s in Wales and elsewhere in the United Kingdom. Although Welsh Springers were recognized by the AKC® in 1906, it is still a relatively uncommon breed in the United States. They were originally bred to "spring" game into a net, prior to the widespread use of firearms for hunting. Welsh Springers today are devoted family dogs, excellent hunting companions, and active dogs well suited to agility, obedience, rally, and tracking.

FORM AND FUNCTION

The breed has remained virtually unchanged for one hundred and fifty years, and breeders and owners take great pride that their dogs can work at an AKC® hunting test one day and enter the show ring at a conformation event the next. There is no deviation between working and show types of Welsh Springer. A typical Welsh Springer will range from 17 to 19 inches at the withers (shoulder) and will weigh between 35 to 55 pounds, with females on the smaller side of both ranges. Welsh Springers are bred to be working spaniels, designed to hunt over steep, rocky terrain that is covered with coarse underbrush. As working dogs, they may be considered to lack "glamour" and do not have the profuse coat of some of their spaniel cousins. However, their shiny coat of deep red and brilliant white makes them beautiful dogs who turn heads wherever they go. Most owners get used to hearing, "That's a beautiful dog. What kind is it?" And the dogs never get tired of the attention.

LIVING WITH A WELSH SPRINGER

The Welsh Springer tends to be "reserved with strangers," to quote the breed standard. This should not be taken to mean a Welsh Springer is timid or shy. When meeting with breeders, be aware that Welsh puppies may take time to warm up to you and your family. But, given time, they should be inquisitive and happy to be touched and picked up. If exposed to children at an early age, Welsh are excellent companions for a young and growing family. Keep in mind that they are hunting dogs, and the urge to chase birds and small mammals has been bred into them for hundreds of years. Most puppies learn quickly to respect your housecat or another dog, but in some cases your puppy may require additional training to learn to live peaceably with pet birds or rodents. These are active dogs who are happiest when they have plenty of exercise and time with their people. A securely fenced yard is best, but long daily walks on a leash would also suffice. In fact, your Welsh Springer will prefer a long walk at your side as opposed to sitting alone in the backyard. Interaction with his humans is key to a happy Welsh Springer. An evening spent sprawled across your lap as you read or watch television will quickly become one of your Welsh's favorite things if you give him the chance. Take that opportunity to run a comb or brush through his coat. Although not as profuse as the feathering on some other sporting dogs, Welsh Springers require at least weekly maintenance to keep their coats shiny and free of mats. The Welsh Springer is an excellent choice for those with an active lifestyle, as well as those looking for a loving family companion. Given the opportunity, these lovely spaniels will steal your heart.

COMPETITION

Welsh Springers are active dogs who may compete and earn titles in conformation, field trials, hunting tests, obedience, rally, agility, tracking, and coursing ability test. A deeply bred desire to please people also makes the Welsh an excellent therapy dog.

Official Standard for the Welsh Springer Spaniel

General Appearance: The Welsh Springer Spaniel is a dog of distinct variety and ancient origin, who derives his name from his hunting style and not his relationship to other breeds. He is an attractive dog of handy size, exhibiting substance without coarseness. He is compact, not leggy, obviously built for hard work and endurance. The Welsh Springer Spaniel gives the impression of length due to obliquely angled forequarters and well developed hindquarters. Being a hunting dog, he should be shown in hard muscled working condition. His coat should not be so excessive as to hinder his work as an active flushing spaniel, but should be thick enough to protect him from heavy cover and weather.

Size, Proportion, Substance: A dog is ideally 18 to 19 inches in height at the withers and a bitch is 17 to 18 inches at the withers. Any animal above or below the ideal to be proportionately penalized. Weight should be in proportion to height and overall balance. Length of body from the withers to the base of the tail is very slightly greater than the distance from the withers to the ground. This body length may be the same as the height but never shorter, thus preserving the rectangular silhouette of the Welsh Springer Spaniel.

Head: The Welsh Springer Spaniel head is unique and should in no way approximate that of other spaniel breeds. Its overall balance is of primary importance. Head is in proportion to body, never so broad as to appear coarse nor so narrow as to appear racy. The skull is of medium length, slightly domed, with a clearly defined stop. It is well chiseled below the eyes. The top plane of the skull is very slightly divergent from that of the muzzle, but with no tendency toward a down-faced appearance. A short chubby head is most objectionable.

Eyes should be oval in shape, dark to medium brown in color with a soft expression. Preference is for

Welsh Springer Spaniel

a darker eye though lighter shades of brown are acceptable. Yellow or mean-looking eyes are to be heavily penalized. Medium in size, they are neither prominent, nor sunken, nor do they show haw. Eye rims are tight and dark pigmentation is preferred. *Ears* are set on approximately at eye level and hang close to the cheeks. Comparatively small, the leather does not reach to the nose. Gradually narrowing toward the tip, they are shaped somewhat like a vine leaf and are lightly feathered.

The length of the *muzzle* is approximately equal to, but never longer than that of the skull. It is straight, fairly square, and free from excessive flew. Nostrils are well developed and black or any shade of brown in color. A pink nose is to be severely penalized. A scissors *bite* is preferred. An undershot jaw is to be severely penalized.

Neck, Topline, Body: The *neck* is long and slightly arched, clean in throat, and set into long, sloping shoulders. *Topline* is level. The loin is slightly arched, muscular, and close-coupled. The croup is very slightly rounded, never steep nor falling off. The topline in combination with proper angulation fore and aft presents a silhouette that appears rectangular. The *chest* is well developed and muscular with a prominent forechest, the ribs well sprung and the brisket reaching to the elbows. The *tail* is an extension of the topline. Carriage is nearly horizontal or slightly elevated when the dog is excited. The tail is generally docked and displays a lively action.

Forequarters: The shoulder blade and upper arm are approximately equal in length. The upper arm is set well back, joining the shoulder blade with sufficient angulation to place the elbow beneath the highest point of the shoulder blade when standing. The forearms are of medium length, straight and moderately feathered. The legs are well boned but not to the extent of coarseness. The Welsh Springer Spaniel's elbows should be close to the body and its pasterns short and slightly sloping. Height to the elbows is approximately equal to the distance

from the elbows to the top of the shoulder blades. Dewclaws are generally removed. Feet should be round, tight and well arched with thick pads.

Hindquarters: The hindquarters must be strong, muscular, and well boned, but not coarse. When viewed in profile the thighs should be wide and the second thighs well developed. The angulation of the pelvis and femur corresponds to that of the shoulder and upper arm. Bend of stifle is moderate. The bones from the hocks to the pads are short with a well angulated hock joint. When viewed from the side or rear they are perpendicular to the ground. Rear dewclaws are removed. Feet as in front.

Coat: The coat is naturally straight flat and soft to the touch, never wiry or wavy. It is sufficiently dense to be waterproof, thornproof, and weatherproof. The back of the forelegs, the hind legs above the hocks, chest and underside of the body are moderately feathered. The ears and tail are lightly feathered. Coat so excessive as to be a hindrance in the field is to be discouraged. Obvious barbering is to be avoided as well.

Color: The color is rich red and white only. Any pattern is acceptable and any white area may be flecked with red ticking.

Gait: The Welsh Springer moves with a smooth, powerful, ground covering action that displays drive from the rear. Viewed from the side, he exhibits a strong forward stride with a reach that does not waste energy. When viewed from the front, the legs should appear to move forward in an effortless manner with no tendency for the feet to cross over or interfere with each other. Viewed from the rear, the hocks should follow on a line with the forelegs, neither too widely nor too closely spaced. As the speed increases the feet tend to converge towards a center line.

Temperament: The Welsh Springer Spaniel is an active dog displaying a loyal and affectionate disposition. Although reserved with strangers, he is not timid, shy nor unfriendly. To this day he remains a devoted family member and hunting companion.

Approved June 13, 1989
Effective August 1, 1989

Meet the Wirehaired Pointing Griffon

Recognized by AKC® in 1887
American Wirehaired Pointing Griffon Association (awpga.com), formed in 1991

Traits
- Intelligent
- Social
- Devoted

HISTORY

The story of today's Wirehaired Pointing Griffon starts in 1874, when Dutch sportsman Eduard K. Korthals decided to create a versatile hunting dog possessing a keen game-finding nose and a steady point with the ability to track and retrieve downed game on land or from water. In less than twenty years, Korthals succeeded in creating the ideal, robust hunting companion with a swift and efficient ground-covering stride and the endurance for an all-day hunt. In 1887, the breed standard was published, and the international Griffon Club in Europe was formed. That same year, the first Griffon arrived in the United States, a direct descendant from one of Korthals's original dogs. In 1916, the Griffon Club of America was formed, but two World Wars interrupted its activities. With renewed interest, the Wirehaired Pointing Griffon Club of America was formed in 1951. During the 1980s, this club decided to crossbreed the Cesky Fousek (a rare Czech gun dog) with the WPG. The American Wirehaired Pointing Griffon Association, formed in 1991 and recognized by the AKC® as the official parent club, remains dedicated to the purebred Griffon.

FORM AND FUNCTION

The modern WPG still possesses the qualities that Korthals envisioned over a century ago. He is a medium-sized dog with a functional double coat and distinctive facial furnishings. A versatile gun dog with a high degree of trainability, the Griffon excels in hunting upland birds, waterfowl, and furred game. He is a deliberate, thorough, and tireless worker with a strong desire to please his master. This sporting dog needs plenty of exercise to keep him physically and mentally fit. The Griffon is a loyal, affectionate family companion and is easily adaptable to any task his master asks him to perform.

LIVING WITH A GRIFFON

When selecting a puppy, it is important to find a responsible breeder who will welcome your inquiring about his or her dogs. Conscientious breeders will screen their breeding stock for potential genetic diseases. Griffons are social animals who require a good deal of attention, consistent training, time, and patience. Griffons do not make good full-time kennel dogs. They are especially active as puppies and are very intelligent, social, and physically powerful as adults. They require considerable mental and physical challenges on a daily basis, or they can become bored, unhappy, and/or destructive. The ideal Griffon household is one where the people are active and include the dog in their daily routines. A Griffon whose mental, emotional, and physical needs are met on a daily basis can be an exceptionally pleasant and easy-to-live-with companion.

The minimally shedding Griffon coat has a harsh outer layer with a soft, insulating undercoat. These dogs require weekly brushing or combing, regular nail trimming, and tooth brushing, as well as occasional trimming around the feet and ears. Some coats may need to be hand-stripped periodically to encourage growth of new coat. Like all dogs with drop ears, a Griffon's ears are susceptible to infections, so regular cleaning and plucking of ear canal hair are recommended.

COMPETITION

Always eager to please, the Griffon makes an ideal partner in competition. The WPG is eligible to participate in numerous AKC® events including conformation, pointing-breed field trials, obedience, agility, rally, tracking, and hunting tests for both pointing dogs and retrievers.

Official Standard for the Wirehaired Pointing Griffon

General Appearance: Medium sized, with a noble, square-shaped head, strong of limb, bred to cover all terrain encountered by the walking hunter. Movement showing an easy catlike gracefulness.

Excels equally as a pointer in the field, or a retriever in the water. Coat is hard and coarse, never curly or woolly, with a thick undercoat of fine hair, giving an unkempt appearance. His easy trainability, devotion to family, and friendly temperament endear him to all. The nickname of "supreme gun dog" is well earned.

Size, Proportion, Substance: *Size*—22 to 24 inches for males, 20 to 22 inches for females. Correct size is important. Oversize to be *severely penalized.* *Proportion*—Slightly longer than tall, in a ratio of 10 to 9. Height from withers to ground; length from point of shoulder to point of buttocks. The Griffon must not evolve towards a square conformation. *Substance* medium, reflecting his work as an all-terrain hunting dog.

Head: The *head* is to be in proportion to the overall dog. The *skull* is of medium width with equal length from nose to stop and from stop to occiput. The skull is slightly rounded on top, but from the side the *muzzle* and head are square. The *stop* and *occiput* are only slightly pronounced. The required abundant mustache and eyebrows contribute to the friendly *expression*. The *eyes* are large and well open, more rounded than elliptical. They have an alert, friendly, and intelligent expression. Eye color ranges in all shades of yellow and brown. Haws should not show nor should there be protruding eyes. The *ears* should be of medium size, lying flat and close to the head, set high, at the height of the eye line. *Nose*—Well open nostrils are essential. Nose color is always brown. Any other color is a *disqualification.* *Bite* scissors. Overshot or undershot bite is a *serious fault.*

Neck, Topline, Body: *Neck*—Rather long, slightly arched, no dewlap. *Topline*—The back is strong and firm, descending in a gentle slope from the slightly higher withers to the base of the tail. *Body*— *Chest*—The *chest* must descend to the level of the elbow, with a moderate spring of rib. The chest must neither be too wide nor too narrow, but of medium width to allow freedom of movement. The *loin* is strong and well developed, being of medium length.

The croup and rump are stoutly made with adequate length to favor speed. The **tail** extends from the back in a continuation of the topline. It may be carried straight or raised slightly. It is docked by one-third to one-half length.

Forequarters: *Shoulders* are long, with good angulation, and well laid back. The *forelegs* are straight and vertical from the front and set well under the shoulder from the side. *Pasterns* are slightly sloping. Dewclaws should be removed. *Feet* are round, firm, with tightly closed webbed toes. Pads are thick.

Hindquarters: The *thighs* are long and well muscled. Angulation in balance with the front. The *legs* are vertical with the hocks turning neither in nor out. The *stifle* and *hock joints* are strong and well angulated. *Feet* as in front.

Coat: The coat is one of the distinguishing features of the breed. It is a double coat. The outer coat is medium length, straight and wiry, never curly or woolly. The harsh texture provides protection in rough cover. The obligatory undercoat consists of a fine, thick down, which provides insulation as well as water resistance. The undercoat is more or less abundant, depending upon the season, climate, and hormone cycle of the dog. It is usually lighter in color. The head is furnished with a prominent mustache and eyebrows. These required features are extensions of the undercoat, which gives the Griffon a somewhat untidy appearance. The hair covering the ears is fairly short and soft, mixed with longer harsh hair from the coat. The overall feel is much less wiry than the body. The legs, both front and rear, are covered with denser, shorter, and less coarse hair. The coat on the tail is the same as the body; any type of plume is prohibited. The breed should be exhibited in full body coat, not stripped short in pattern. Trimming and stripping are only allowed around the ears, top of head, cheeks and feet.

Color: Preferably steel gray with brown markings, frequently chestnut brown, or roan, white and brown; white and orange also acceptable. A uniformly brown coat, all white coat, or white and orange are less desirable. A black coat *disqualifies*.

Gait: Although close working, the Griffon should cover ground in an efficient, tireless manner. He is a medium-speed dog with perfect coordination between front and rear legs. At a trot, both front and rear legs tend to converge toward the center line of gravity. He shows good extension both front and rear. Viewed from the side, the topline is firm and parallel to the line of motion. A smooth, powerful ground-covering ability can be seen.

Temperament: The Griffon has a quick and intelligent mind and is easily trained. He is outgoing, shows a tremendous willingness to please and is trustworthy. He makes an excellent family dog as well as a meticulous hunting companion.

Disqualifications: *Nose any color other than brown. Black coat.*

Approved October 8, 1991
Effective November 28, 1991

Meet the Wirehaired Vizsla

Recognized by AKC® in 2014
Wirehaired Vizsla Club of America (wvca.club), formed in 2003

Traits
- Happy
- Gentle
- Loyal

HISTORY

The Wirehaired Vizsla was developed in the region of the former Austria-Hungary during the years between the World Wars. Hunters and falconers wanted a dog like the Vizsla, but sturdier, with a thick wiry coat that would be resistant to their harsh winters and field conditions. They began with two Vizsla bitches and a solid-brown German Wirehaired Pointer dog. They persisted in the preservation and development of the breed throughout World War II and its aftermath. The Wirehaired Vizsla was recognized in Europe by the Fédération Cynologique Internationale (FCI) in 1966.

Although recognized by the Canadian Kennel Club in 1977, the Wirehaired Vizsla remained obscure in the United States due to an early identity crisis. A pair was imported in 1973, after someone discovered the breed in earlier visits to Hungary, but he called them "Uplanders," from their origins in the uplands of northern Hungary. He formed a club and applied for recognition in the Field Dog Stud Book and AKC®. There were far too few, and, because they weren't recognized as Uplanders anywhere else, registries would not recognize them by that name. Efforts to promote Uplanders died out, and few records remain.

Supporters of the breed in America persisted in their efforts to preserve the integrity of the purebred Wirehaired Vizsla, continuing to import purebred registered European stock for their breeding programs. The Wirehaired Vizsla Club of America was formed in 2003 and was approved for AKC®'s Foundation Stock Service® on January 1, 2008. The breed entered the Sporting Group in 2014.

FORM AND FUNCTION

Balanced in size and proportion, the Wirehaired Vizsla is a lean, athletic hunting dog of medium size. Sturdy and strong, he is powerful yet graceful, with

AKC Official Guide to Sporting Dogs

a far-reaching drive that enables him to hunt in all elements and cover any terrain encountered by the walking hunter. He has a keen nose for hunting and tracking feather and fur, on land and in water, as well as a natural point and retrieve. Strong natural swimmers, most Wirehaired Vizslas love to get in the water and will at every opportunity. The breed's most distinguishing features are its weather-resistant, dense wire coat and furnishings, including beard, eyebrows, and brushes on the legs. From nose and eyes to toenails, the Wirehaired Vizsla is self-colored in harmony with his coat of golden rust.

LIVING WITH A WIREHAIRED VIZSLA

A Wirehaired Vizsla's temperament should be happy and confident, so always look for a puppy who is friendly and outgoing, inquisitive, and willing to explore his surroundings. If selecting a puppy for show or for hunting, be aware that his coat may be very different at eight weeks than it will be as a mature adult. That cute fuzzy puppy is liable to have a soft coat that is longer than desirable, whereas a puppy with a coat that is sleek and short may take up to two or even three years to develop a wire coat and furnishings. Look for just a hint of bushy eyebrows and beard to come; the amount of hair around the pads of the feet is another good indicator of the amount of coat to expect—the fuzzier the undersides of the feet are, the heavier the coat will be.

The ideal owner for the breed is someone who wants a dog to live in his or her home and be included in family activities, especially outdoors. Wirehaired Vizslas are athletic and intelligent, needing plenty of exercise and mental stimulation. They are happiest with a job to do, eager to please and easy to train using positive methods. Owners need a light but firm hand in discipline; a Wirehaired Vizsla needs structure and boundaries, or he could rule the house. The dog's soft temperament does not require harsh words or severe physical punishment. Wirehaired Vizslas have a strong bond with their families and can develop separation anxiety without proper conditioning. Their coats require regular brushing and an occasional bath, and periodic stripping is necessary to remove old dead hair and allow new wiry hair to grow. Beards can be wet and messy, so keep a towel handy to dry a hairy face.

COMPETITION

Wirehaired Vizslas can compete in conformation and all companion events, including obedience, agility, rally, and tracking, as well as in hunting tests for pointing breeds. The Wirehaired Vizsla can also compete in flyball, urban search and rescue, and Barn Hunt.

Official Standard for the Wirehaired Vizsla

General Appearance: Originating in Hungary, the Wirehaired Vizsla was developed by hunters and falconers who desired a sturdy, versatile hunting dog able to withstand harsh winters in the field, forest and water. The Wirehaired Vizsla is a distinguished, versatile hunting dog of medium size, bred for substance and a dense wire coat. Balanced in size and proportion, the Wirehaired Vizsla is robust and lean. Movement is powerful yet graceful with far reaching drive enabling the breed to hunt in all elements and cover any terrain encountered by the walking hunter. The breed possesses an excellent nose for hunting and tracking feather and fur on land and in water, as well as a natural point and retrieve. The breed's most distinguishing features are its weather resistant dense wire coat and its facial furnishings, specifically its beard and eyebrows. Natural appearance is essential to breed type, therefore the Wirehaired Vizsla is to be shown with limited stripping and should not be penalized for being shown in working condition: sinewy, well muscled, with honorable scars. The Wirehaired Vizsla is intelligent, loyal, sensitive and biddable, but cannot tolerate harsh handling. Eager to learn, lively yet gentle, they are readily trainable for gun and falcon. The Wirehaired Vizsla is a tractable and affectionate companion in the home.

Size, Proportion, Substance: The Wirehaired Vizsla is a medium-sized hunting dog, however overall symmetry and balance are more important than mere measurable size. The ideal male adult (over 12 months of age) is 23 to 25 inches at the highest point over the shoulder blades. The ideal female adult (over 12 months of age) is 21½ to 23 inches. Because the Wirehaired Vizsla is meant to be a medium-sized hunter, any dog measuring more than 1 inch over or under these limits must be disqualified. The body length from breastbone to buttocks slightly exceeds the height at the shoulders, as 10 is to 9. The Wirehaired Vizsla body is well muscled and strong, with sufficient bone and substance.

Head: The Wirehaired Vizsla's *head* is in proportion to the body, moderate and well muscled. The *expression* should be lively, clever, and is enhanced by the eyebrows and beard. *Eyes* are slightly oval, of medium size with well fitting eyelids, giving the Wirehaired Vizsla an intelligent and lively expression. Iris color is as dark as possible and blends harmoniously with the coat color. Yellow eyes are a serious fault. Eye rim color should blend with the coat color, but freckles from sun or age are not to be faulted. Lower eye rims should neither turn in nor out. *Ears* are set at a medium height, moderate in length, hanging close to the cheeks and ending in a rounded V shape. The *skull* is well muscled, moderate in length, and slightly domed. A slight groove runs from the moderate occiput to the stop. The stop is moderate. The *muzzle* is slightly shorter than half the length of the head when viewed in profile. The muzzle is blunt, with a straight bridge that is parallel to the top of the skull and is well muscled with strong jaws. The nose is wide with nostrils well open. The nose color should blend with the coat color. Any black on the nose is a disqualification, but brown freckles, due to aging or sun exposure are not to be faulted. The bearded lips lay close to the jaw as tightly as possible. The jaw is strong with teeth aligned in a scissors *bite*. An over or undershot bite or more than two missing teeth is a disqualification.

Neck, Topline, Body: The *neck* is in balance with the body and head, medium in length, muscular and slightly arched. Skin on the neck and body is tight fitting, there is no dewlap. The shoulders are strong and muscular. The *topline* is straight, well muscled and solid, falling into a slightly rounded, well muscled croup, which is moderate in length. The chest is deep, moderately broad, and well muscled.

The depth of the chest is slightly less than half the height at the shoulders and sets at the elbow when seen from the side. The forechest is well developed. The ribs are moderately sprung and carried well back. The underline is graceful with a moderate tuck-up. The loin is tight, well muscled and straight or slightly arched. The tail is set just below the level of the croup. The tail is thick at its base then tapers and carries a dense coat. The preferred tail is docked by one-quarter of its length; natural tails will not be penalized. A natural tail reaches down to the hock joint and is carried straight or slightly saber-like. When moving, the tail is carried near the horizontal, not curled over the back or carried between the legs.

Forequarters: The forequarters are well muscled with strong, sufficient bone and balance. From the front, legs are straight, from the side they are placed well under the body. Shoulders are well laid back, showing fluidity when moving. The upper arm is well muscled, about equal to the shoulder in length and well angulated at its attachment to the shoulder, in order to allow for good extension. The elbows lie close to the body; pasterns are short, sinewy and only very slightly sloping. Preferably, dewclaws are removed from the front legs to avoid injury in the field, but a dog with natural dewclaws is not to be penalized. The feet are cat-like, but slightly oval and always parallel. Pads are thick and tough; nails are self colored and short.

Hindquarters: The hindquarters are straight and parallel with well developed thighs when viewed from behind. The angulation of the hindquarters is in balance with the forequarters. The legs have strong, sufficient bone and balance, with thighs that are well muscled and long. The stifle is well angulated. The hocks are strong, well let down, short and straight as viewed from behind. Rear dewclaws are a disqualification. Feet are as in the Forequarters section.

Coat: The Wirehaired Vizsla's coat makes this breed unique. Close lying, a length of approximately 1 inch, the dense wiry coat should not hide the outline of the body. Functionally the coat should protect against weather and injury with a dense undercoat and wiry outer coat. The lower legs and underside of the chest and belly are covered with shorter, softer, thinner coat. Coat on the head and ears is close fitting and shorter. Pronounced eyebrows highlight the stop.

Expression is enhanced not only by eyebrows, but also by a strong, harsh beard, approximately 1 inch in length, formed from both sides of the muzzle. On both sides of the neck the coat forms V-shaped brushes. Lacking undercoat or coat brushes on the back of the front legs should be penalized, as is any deviation in coat texture or excessive length of the coat. The Wirehaired Vizsla should be exhibited almost in his natural state, nothing more in the way of stripping being needed than a tidying up. A clipped coat is faulty.

Color: Golden rust in varying shades. Red, brown or yellow colors are faulty. The ears may be slightly darker than the body; otherwise the coat color is uniform. White on the forechest or throat, not more than 2 inches in diameter, as well as white on the toes is permissible and common. Solid white extending above the toes or white anywhere else on the dog except the forechest and throat is a disqualification. White due to aging or scars from hunting is not to be faulted. The Wirehaired Vizsla is self-colored, with the color of the eyes, eye rims, lips, nose and toenails blending with the color of the coat.

Gait: The Wirehaired Vizsla should move in a light-footed, smooth trot. When seen from the side, the gait is dynamic yet graceful and there is a balance to the movement with far reaching drive. The topline remains level, the back firm. When working in the field his sound movement enhances his ability as a versatile hunting dog.

Temperament: The Wirehaired Vizsla is self-confident, eager to learn, clever, sensitive and yet stubborn; affectionate and loyal with his owner, occasionally aloof with strangers and has a keen protective instinct. Shyness, nervousness or aggressiveness are faulty.

Disqualifications: *Dogs over 12 months of age measuring over 26 inches or under 22 inches and bitches over 12 months of age over 24 inches or under 20½ inches. Partial or completely black nose. Under or overshot bite. More than two missing teeth. Rear dewclaws. White extending above the toes or white anywhere else on the dog except the forechest and throat. More than 2 inches of white in any direction on the forechest and throat.*

Approved August 18, 2012
Effective January 1, 2013

Index

A

agility tests, about, 20
AKC® Canine Health Foundation (CHF), 8
AKC® Canine Partners, 10
AKC® Education, 9
AKC® Family Dog (magazine), 10
The AKC® Gazette (magazine), 10
AKC® Humane Fund, 9
AKC® Inspections, 9
AKC Meet the Breeds®, 9
AKC® Museum of the Dog, 10
AKC Rally®, 22
AKC® Research Library, 10
AKC® Reunite, 8
AKC Scent Work®, 20–21
AKC.org, 10
AKC.TV, 10
American Kennel Club® (AKC®). *See also* sports and activities
about: origins and overview, 8
building community, 9–10
founding and mission of, 8
health and welfare advancement, 8–9
organizations of, 8–10
American Water Spaniel, **24–27**
anatomy of a dog, 11–13
about: overview of, 11
by breed (*See specific breeds*)
breed standards by body part, 11–13

B

Barbet, **28–31**
bite, general standards, 12. *See also specific breeds*
body parts, breed standards (general), 11–13. *See also specific breeds*
Boykin Spaniel, **32–35**
Bracco Italiano, **36–39**
breeders, choosing/considerations, 16–17

Brittany, **40–43**

C

Canine Good Citizen®/S.T.A.R. Puppy®, 22
Chesapeake Bay Retriever, **44–47**
Clumber Spaniel, **48–51**
coat, standards. *See specific breeds*
Cocker Spaniel, **52–55**
color, standards. *See specific breeds*
community, AKC® building, 9–10
competition. *See specific breeds*; standards by body part
conformation events, 19
Curly-Coated Retriever, 12, **56–59**

D

disqualification criteria. *See specific breeds*

E

ears, general standards, 12. *See also specific breeds*
education, AKC®, 9
English Cocker Spaniel, 16, **60–63**
English Setter, **64–67**
English Springer Spaniel, **68–72**

F

Fast CAT®, 22
faults, by breed. *See specific breeds*
feet, general standards, 13. *See also specific breeds*
Field Spaniel, 11, **73–76**
field trials and hunting tests, 21
Flat-Coated Retriever, 23, **77–80**
forequarters, standards. *See specific breeds*
form and function of breeds. *See specific breeds*
front assembly, general standards, 12–13. *See also specific breeds*

G

gait/movement, standards. *See specific breeds*
German Shorthaired Pointer, 15, 20, **81–84**
German Wirehaired Pointer, **85–88**
Golden Retriever, 14, **89–92**
Gordon Setter, **93–96**
grooming, standards. *See specific breeds*

H

health and welfare, AKC® services, 8–9
hindquarters, standards. *See specific breeds*
history
of the AKC®, 8
of specific breeds (*See specific breeds*)
hunting tests and field trials, 21

I

inspections, AKC®, 9
Irish Red and White Setter, **97–99**
Irish Setter, 10, **100–103**
Irish Water Spaniel, 3, 9, **104–7**

J

Junior Showmanship program, 19

L

Labrador Retriever, 13, **108–13**
Lagotto Romagnolo, **114–18**
living with various breeds. *See specific breeds*
lost pets, reuniting with owners, 9

M

magazines, award-winning, 10
museum, AKC® Museum of the Dog, 10

N

neck, body, topline standards. *See specific breeds*
Nederlandse Kooikerhondje, **119–22**
Nova Scotia Duck Tolling Retriever, 1, **123–26**

O

obedience exercises, 20

P

Pointer, **127–30**. *See also* German Shorthaired Pointer; German Wirehaired Pointer
proportion, size, substance standards. *See specific breeds*
public events, AKC®, 9
puppies, 14–17
    breed selection, 15–16
    breeder considerations, 16–17
    considerations for getting, 15
    S.T.A.R. Puppy®, 22

R

rally, AKC Rally®, 22
rear assembly, general standards, 13. *See also specific breeds*
retrievers. *See* Chesapeake Bay Retriever; Curly-Coated Retriever; Flat-Coated Retriever; Golden Retriever; Labrador Retriever; Nova Scotia Duck Tolling Retriever
reuniting pets with owners, 8
rib cage, general standards, 13. *See also specific breeds*

S

Scent Work, AKC®, 20–21
setters. *See* English Setter; Gordon Setter; Irish Red and White Setter; Irish Setter
size, proportion, substance standards. *See specific breeds*
skin and coat, standards. *See specific breeds*

spaniels. *See* American Water Spaniel; Boykin Spaniel; Clumber Spaniel; Cocker Spaniel; English Cocker Spaniel; English Springer Spaniel; Field Spaniel; Irish Water Spaniel; Sussex Spaniel; Welsh Springer Spaniel
Spinone Italiano, **131–34**
Sporting Group breeds
    about: overview of, 3, 23
    American Water Spaniel, **24–27**
    Barbet, **28–31**
    Boykin Spaniel, **32–35**
    Bracco Italiano, **36–39**
    Brittany, **40–43**
    Chesapeake Bay Retriever, **44–47**
    Clumber Spaniel, **48–51**
    Cocker Spaniel, **52–55**
    Curly-Coated Retriever, 12, **56–59**
    English Cocker Spaniel, 16, **60–63**
    English Setter, **64–67**
    English Springer Spaniel, **68–72**
    Field Spaniel, 11, **73–76**
    Flat-Coated Retriever, 23, **77–80**
    German Shorthaired Pointer, 15, 20, **81–84**
    German Wirehaired Pointer, **85–88**
    Golden Retriever, 14, **89–92**
    Gordon Setter, **93–96**
    Irish Red and White Setter, **97–99**
    Irish Setter, 10, **100–103**
    Irish Water Spaniel, 3, 9, **104–7**
    Labrador Retriever, 3, 13, **108–13**
    Lagotto Romagnolo, **114–18**
    Nederlandse Kooikerhondje, **119–22**
    Nova Scotia Duck Tolling Retriever, 1, **123–26**
    Pointer, **127–30**
    Spinone Italiano, **131–34**
    Sussex Spaniel, **135–38**
    Vizsla, **139–42** (*See also* Wirehaired Vizsla)
    Weimaraner, 4, 22, **143–46**
    Welsh Springer Spaniel, **147–50**
    Wirehaired Pointing Griffon, 8, **151–54**
    Wirehaired Vizsla, **155–58**

sports and activities
    about: history and overview of, 18
    age range of human participants, 19
    agility tests, 20
    AKC Rally®, 22
    Canine Good Citizen®/S.T.A.R. Puppy®, 22
    conformation events, 19
    Fast CAT®, 22
    field trials and hunting tests, 21
    Junior Showmanship program, 19
    obedience exercises, 20
    range of, 18
    standards by body part, 11–13 (*See also specific breeds*)
    tracking and AKC Scent Work®, 20–21
standards by body part, 11–13. *See also specific breeds*
S.T.A.R. Puppy®, 22
substance, size, proportions standards. *See specific breeds*
Sussex Spaniel, **135–38**

T

tails, general standards, 13. *See also specific breeds*
temperament, standards. *See specific breeds*
tracking and AKC Scent Work®, 20–21
traits by breed. *See specific breeds*
TV, AKC.TV, 10

V

Vizsla, **139–42**. *See also* Wirehaired Vizsla

W

website, *AKC. org*, 10
Weimaraner, 4, 22, **143–46**
Welsh Springer Spaniel, **147–50**
Wirehaired Pointing Griffon, 8, **151–54**
Wirehaired Vizsla, **155–58**